PICTORIAL HOOKED RUGS

Old Mill on the Eastern Shore, *14" x 12", #3- to 5-cut, wool on linen. Designed and hooked by Jane Halliwell Green, Edgewater, Maryland, 2008.*

PICTORIAL HOOKED RUGS

JANE HALLIWELL GREEN

DEDICATION

I dedicate this book to John and Catherine Halliwell, two special parents who nurtured my passion for creativity and self expression. I am eternally grateful for their presence in my life.

Special thanks to my wonderful children, Kate and Marc Senger, and to my loving husband, Don Green, who pitched in to help me edit and create the illustrations for this manuscript.

Lastly, I send my love to my rug hooking students. Thanks for your support, creativity, and sense of humor that never ends. You have given this rug hooker many happy moments, and I hope there will be many more to come!

Front Cover: Detail from The Way the Faeries Went, *27" x 46", #3-cut wool on linen. Designed and hooked by Jane Halliwell Green, Edgewater, Maryland, 1999. Photographed by Donald Green.*

Back Cover Rug: Sunflower Cottage, *13" x 11", #3- and 4-cut on cotton warp cloth. Designed and hooked by Jane Halliwell Green, Edgewater, Maryland, 2008.*

Copyright© 2009 by Stackpole Books

Published by
STACKPOLE BOOKS
5067 Ritter Road
Mechanicsburg, PA 17055
www.stackpolebooks.com

Printed in Fulton, Missouri

10 9 8 7 6 5 4 3 2 1

First edition

Cover design by Caroline Stover
Photography by Jane Halliwell Green, unless otherwise noted

Library of Congress Cataloging-in-Publication Data

Green, Jane Halliwell.
    Pictorial Hooked Rugs / Jane Halliwell Green.—1st ed.
    p. cm.
    Includes bibliographical references.

    ISBN: 978-1-881982-66-1;
1. Rugs, Hooked. 2. Fabric pictures. I. Title.
    TT850.G65 2009
    746.7'041—dc22

Canadian GST #R137954772

CONTENTS

Nubble Light, 16" x 20", #3- and 4-cut wool on cotton warp cloth. Karlkraft pattern available through Harry M. Fraser Company. Hooked by Pamela Manders, Annapolis, Maryland, 2008.

ACKNOWLEDGMENTS

I am deeply grateful to all the wonderful rug artists who allowed me to share their work on these pages. Pictorial rugs are personal memories and events depicted in fiber. I am certain these works of art will inspire many rug hookers in the future to pick up the hook for the first time and have the courage to express themselves in this beautiful medium.

JoAnne Bailey
Marjorie Barnard
Mary Lou Bleakley
Kathleen Bush
Pamela Brune
Sally D' Albora
Sheri DeMate
Claire deRoos
Peggy Dutton
Lynne Fowler
Alice Fraizer
Donald Green
Mary Beth Hawks
Sally and Richard Henderson
JoAnn Hendrix
Kathy Hottenstein

Roslyn Logsdon
Pamela Manders
Nancy Maclennan
Janet Matthews
Irene Michaud
Louise Miller
Cyndra Mogayzel
Nancy Parcels
Sarah Province
Kate Senger
Dorothy Sexton
Susie Stephenson
Fran Trischman
Sue Welch
Lissa Williamson

Finally, I would like to thank Ginny Stimmel for her expert guidance throughout this project and for giving me the opportunity to write another book about my favorite subject.

ABOUT THE AUTHOR

Jane Halliwell Green began hooking rugs when she was ten years old at the urging of her Irish grandmother. An unfinished rug always stood at the entrance to her grandmother's New England home, and the only way she and the other grandchildren were allowed passage into the kitchen was to hook a few loops. It was years later, in 1988, that she remembered her grandmother's rugs and fell in love with the art of rug hooking again. She drove long distances to study with McGown teachers, and in 1993 Jane became a certified McGown teacher herself.

Jane teaches classes and workshops in the United States and Canada and was the first rug hooking instructor to teach at the Smithsonian Institute in Washington, DC. She served on the editorial board of *Rug Hooking* magazine for many years and contributed many articles for publication. She wrote the book, *The Pictorial Rug*, published by Stackpole Books in 2000. That same year she was invited to appear on the Carol DuVal Show on Home and Garden Television. In 2002 she returned to school, and in 2005 she graduated from the Ringling School of Art and Design in Sarasota, Florida, with a Certificate of Fine Arts.

Jane's specialties are pictorial rugs and rugs made with 1"-wide strips, referred to as "close-up rugs." She extensively researched the science of color combinations and developed her own color-planning tools and dye formulas. She sells hand-dyed wools, called "artist wools," to rug hookers in the United States and Canada.

Jane lives in Edgewater, Maryland, with her husband, Don. They have five grown children. She teaches locally at Anne Arundel Community College; Chesapeake College; the Fairfax, Virginia, school system; the Chesapeake Arts Center; and she travels around the country to teach rug hooking. Jane is an accomplished painter and signature member of the Baltimore Watercolor Society.

Visit her web sites at *www.rugandwool.com* and *www.paintpencil.com*.

The Way the Faeries Went, *27" x 46", #3-cut wool on linen. Designed and hooked by Jane Halliwell Green, Edgewater, Maryland, 1999. Photograph by Donald Green, 2009.*

FROM THE EDITOR

One of the most popular requests of rug hookers is for help in designing and hooking realistic pictorial rugs. Learning how to hook different elements, such as brick, stone, sidewalks, and buildings to make them appear realistic is tricky. Author Jane Halliwell Green breaks the process down with easy-to-follow information and step-by-step directions. In this book, she tells you how to pick a subject, create a pattern, and portray perspective. She helps you determine just which elements to include and gives tips on depth perception, color planning, and dye formulas—everything you need to create your own rug from start to finish. *Pictorial Hooked Rugs* closes with an index of dye formulas used throughout the book and an index of the most helpful techniques you will need to produce lovely pictorial rugs of your own.

For a good look at what rug hookers are doing with this fascinating craft, pick up a copy of *Rug Hooking* magazine or visit our web site at *www.rughookingmagazine.com*. There are rugs here for every persuasion from a growing community of giving, gracious fiber artists who will welcome you to their gatherings.—*Ginny Stimmel*

ABOUT THE PUBLISHER

Rug Hooking magazine welcomes you to the rug hooking community. Since 1989 *Rug Hooking* has served thousands of rug hookers around the world with its instructional, illustrated articles on dyeing, designing, color planning, hooking techniques, and more. Each issue of the magazine contains color photographs of beautiful rugs old and new, profiles of teachers, designers, and fellow rug hookers, and announcements of workshops, exhibits, and gatherings.

Rug Hooking has responded to its readers' demands for more inspiration and information by establishing an inviting, informative website at *www.rughookingmagazine.com* and by publishing a number of books on this fiber art. Along with how-to pattern books, *Rug Hooking* has produced the competition-based book series *Celebration of Hand-Hooked Rugs*, now in its 20th year.

The hand-hooked rugs you'll see in *Celebration of Hand-Hooked Rugs XIX* represent just a fragment of the incredible art that is being produced today by women and men of all ages. For more information on rug hooking and *Rug Hooking* magazine, call or write to us at the address on the copyright page.

INTRODUCTION

My first experience planning a pictorial rug was a difficult one. My instructor told me that this was nothing more than a scrap rug and anyone could hook one. Nothing is further from the truth. A pictorial rug is a true work of art and requires some study of the basic principles of art. With that in mind I wrote my first book, *The Pictorial Rug: Everything You Need to Know to Hook a Realistic, Impressionistic, or Primitive Picture with Wool* (Stackpole Books, 2000). The book filled a need and quickly sold out. Rug hookers have been demanding a new one ever since, and I am pleased to present you with a new look at my favorite style of fiber art.

There is a resurgence of interest in pictorial rugs, perhaps because they are, more than any other style, the personal expressions of the individuals who create them. My goal is to build upon the wonderful design ideas of my predecessors and, at the same time, add new techniques to the rug hooker's toolbox.

This book is a real how-to book, divided into color, technique, and dyeing sections. I have taught and studied this form of rug hooking for many years, and I understand your needs. Just as rug hooking has grown and exploded with creativity and new techniques, this new book offers innovative methods for adding a special three-dimensional look to your work.

I present not only the way to achieve a particular result, but also techniques that reflect my style and form of instruction. Some of the terminology used is my own invention created throughout my teaching career.

I hope that rug hookers will find this book useful as a guide and a reference. I hope that when you complete your masterpiece you will proclaim that hooking your pictorial was like reading a good book, and it was such a wonderful experience that you were sorry to see it end.
—*Jane Halliwell Green*

Winter Wonderland, 18" x 16", #3-cut, wool, yarn, and woven fabric on cotton warp cloth. Designed by Jane McGown Flynn. Hooked by Jane Halliwell Green, Edgewater, Maryland, 2001.

CHAPTER 1

Artistic Nuts and Bolts

OUR ANCESTORS' FOOTSTEPS

Capturing the important parts of our lives in pictures is instinctive for us. Pictorial scenes have been created with fiber for centuries. During medieval times, large tapestries were commissioned by the king, and some of these, often with religious significance, can be seen in museums all over the world. In the United States during the 18th century, an important part of a girl's education was to meticulously stitch samplers. The samplers often featured architectural details, as well as brief messages and dates.

Primitive pictorial hooked rugs appeared in the early part of the 19th century at about the same time jute was imported to the United States.* While these early rugs had a simplistic style, they provided insight into the everyday lives of their makers. Their designs included objects of importance to the rug hooker, such as the family homestead, boats, and farm animals. Rarely did landscape scenes appear without some architectural elements. As the century progressed, pictorial rugs contained more and more detail, and storytelling rugs—those that conveyed a message as well as a picture—became popular.

Grenfell rugs, or pictorial rugs hooked with silk hosiery in a distinctive straight row fashion, were created in the early 20th century in the isolated villages of Newfoundland and Labrador. These rugs, which were referred to as "mats," contained scenes of daily maritime life and were sold through Dr. Wilfred Grenfell's mission to improve the living conditions of the local people.

This book is about the pictorial rug of the 21st century, with an emphasis on new techniques to achieve a work of art with fabric. The pictorial rug encompasses such a broad range of themes that it is almost easier to

state what it does not include. A pictorial is not an Oriental, crewel, geometric, or floral design, but it is everything else. A pictorial scene can include floral, geometric, and Oriental motifs—often appearing in the border area. A pictorial is crashing waves on the beaches of Cape Cod; busy city streets; unloading the lobsters on a fishing boat in Portland, Maine; a group of people eating dinner; shoes lying on the floor; a prosperous harbor....

These myriad depictions can be hooked in four styles: primitive, realistic, impressionistic, and stylistic. The primitive and impressionistic styles fall in the center. The stylistic leans close toward abstraction, and the realistic style captures every detail of the picture.

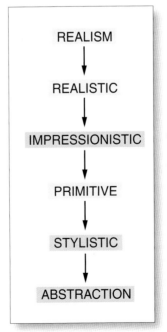

REALISM
↓
REALISTIC
↓
IMPRESSIONISTIC
↓
PRIMITIVE
↓
STYLISTIC
↓
ABSTRACTION

A continuum of pictorial rug styles shows where each style stands in relation to the other styles.

*Jute is a crude type of burlap imported from India.

Graduation Day, 33" x 24", #3- to 7-cut wool on linen. Adapted from a painting by Sharon Eyres. Hooked by Nancy Parcels, Mechanicsburg, Pennsylvania, 2008.

Primitive

The primitive style has been around the longest and is still, in my opinion, the most popular within the rug hooking community. The old hooked pictorials are sought after and valued highly. The makers were untrained artists who told us the stories of their lives in wool. If you have never hooked a pictorial, it is a good idea to begin with the primitive style. It is childlike, bold, and one-dimensional with little attention to scale or perspective. Shape is much more important than scale. The colors can be bright, unlike the faded hues we associate with antique rugs. The maker wants to capture the essence of a scene or moment without attention to detail. Often the right choice of fabric is all the detail you need to get a particular effect. It is the most unrestricted form of rug hooking. A primitive rug's strips are wide ($1/4"$ to $1/2"$), which hastens the hooking process. The use of textured wools predominates. It is perfectly acceptable to outline and fill most of the objects in the design. However, do not be fooled into thinking that hooking a primitive rug is a mindless undertaking. It is, in fact, a style that requires careful planning of composition and color.

Nancy Parcel's delightful primitive rug, *Graduation Day* (page 2), is a good example of color planning and composition. Nancy used leftover bits of wool, or "noodles," to hook the entire rug. She comments that choosing the correct light, medium, and dark values of color for the trees, schoolhouse, and figures was the most difficult part of hooking this piece.

Portland Head Lighthouse, 24" x 31", framed, #3-cut wool on linen. Designed by Pearl McGown. Hooked by Pamela Brune, Odenton, Maryland, 2000.

England Memory Rug,
30" x 70", #5- to #9-cut wool
on monk's cloth. Designed by
Keith Kemmer. Hooked by
Alice Fraizer, Lexington, Ohio,
2007.

TACKLING A PROJECT

Now that you are beginning to think about your own project and the category into which it fits, let's explore the fundamentals of preparing and tackling this pictorial project. Don't be intimidated by the fundamentals. What follows will help you with any style of pictorial you choose. Read the chapter, use it as a guide, and try to incorporate some of the information into your work as you go forward.

The origin of design ideas

Thinking through a design and utilizing the fundamental rules of art can be difficult for many rug hookers. The desire to execute a design quickly so that the hooking can begin immediately is an overwhelming urge. It is very important to practice patience. As with any element of a pictorial scene, the key to a successful interpretation lies in carefully planning each action before picking up a hook. Remember that it is not necessary to have a degree in art to create good

composition or a great work of art. Just follow the simple steps below. The reason pictorial designs fall into the category of sophisticated and challenging rugs will become evident in this chapter.

Choose to hook something you love. You will be living with your project for weeks or months, and a high level of motivation is necessary to bring it to conclusion. The quality of the work and the completion of the project are often tied to your initial level of interest. Ideas are all around you, but select something you know well and feel emotionally tied to. Bring your camera on your travels to interesting places. Take lots of pictures. Early morning and late afternoon shots will give you the most interesting contrasts between light and shadow.

England Memory Rug is a perfect example of a rug inspired by a vacation. Alice Fraizer traveled to England with a large group of rug hookers. Keith Kemmer, a member of the group, designed the rug with vignettes of memorable places. Alice

can make some parts of it light and some areas dark. Tombow pens are available through most large art supply companies. A supplier for the pens is listed in the resource section.

Look for an emotional tie-in. Many of the objects in pictorial design bring forth an emotional response and are attention-getting subjects. People, birds, and animals suggest companionship; doors and windows stir curiosity; artificial lights at night or in the rain are warm and inviting; mailboxes, rocking chairs, and baby carriages bring forth nostalgic sentiments; and patriotic or religious symbols such as flags, steeples, and crosses arouse emotion.

Working from photographs

Photos are a helpful resource, and books have been written on the subject. You can't make an exact copy of a photo because photos never yield a 100 percent accurate representation of any scene. Walls and angles generally have a tendency to lean inward, so they need to be adjusted. Also, film and digital pictures cannot cope with a broad spectrum of light intensity, so you need to take multiple shots using different exposures to get an approximate idea of color, light, and shadow. When working with photos keep these tips in mind:

- Take your own photos because this is the first opportunity to make design decisions. Someone else's photos cannot possibly have the same emotional significance to you.
- Take lots of photos, more than you think you will ever need.
- Keep a photo file. Divide this file into categories such as boats, windows, lakes, skies, flowers, etc.
- Photograph parts of things: clouds, fences, rocks, shadows, parts of buildings, close-ups of windows, and architectural details such as porch rails and trim.
- When designing from a photo, mix in objects from other shots. Try cutting and pasting a picture together to create a new composition, but watch for consistency of light and shadow.

hooked the piece with the help of Barbara Carroll, who produced the patterns for the group. Alice did a fabulous job handling a wide range of pictorial elements from the Durham Cathedral to the brick cottages at Beamish (a re-created old town).

Keep a notebook. Jot down everything you love, and include your own sketches, clippings of interest, Christmas cards, postcards, flower seed catalogs, calendars, and photos. I call this my "idea file" because it is a ready source of design ideas. Consider the story you want to tell. Some individuals simply want to re-create a place they remember fondly as a child. They work from old photographs and memories.

Head outdoors, do some sketching, and collect ideas. Tombow pens, with water-soluble ink and fine and thick points, are good tools for sketching and value studies. You can make a quick sketch by dipping a small brush into a bottle of water, wetting the ink, and dragging it into the drawing. As you brush the ink over the drawing you

Lighthouses, 37¹/₂" round, #3- and 4-cut wool on cotton warp cloth. Designed and hooked by Lissa Williamson, Severna Park, Maryland, 2000.

■ Eliminate detail! Simplify!

■ Once you have a drawing based on a photo, get rid of the photo. Let your creativity and artistic sense lead the way rather than being tempted to copy.

Nancy Parcels, a rug hooking teacher in Mechanicsburg, Pennsylvania, has a wonderful tip about using photographs. She photographs her work as the rug progresses and stores them in flip books. Nancy likes to see her work develop and feels that the photos allow her to catch and correct mistakes sooner.

Other visual references

In addition to your own photos and books, another inexpensive source of reference material is the Internet. Be careful though—most photographs and other works of art on the Internet are copyrighted. This means you cannot copy the work exactly and then call the finished product your own. Here are some good Web sites:

■ *www.Artmorgue.com.* You'll find thousands of reference photos here, including architecture, animals, flowers, clothes, clouds, and nature in general.

- *www.flowers.vg.* Buying fresh flowers in the winter can be a challenge, so this free site is a wonderful resource.
- *www.Art.com.* Photographers and fine artists sell their work on this site. The landscape section will give you lots of ideas, but do not copy—be inspired instead.
- *www.Image.kind.* Artists also sell work on this site.

The road map to design—first decisions

Whether you create your own design or work from a preprinted pattern, take the time to think through all steps—from composition to color—before you pull up your first loop. Skipping this step would be like walking into a room full of people talking a foreign language and not understanding a thing that is said.

Composition

A composition is made up of elements such as shapes, lines, values, sizes, color, and texture. A good composition is a planned arrangement of these elements.

Rug or wall hanging. Once you have a subject for your design, address the first question: will I be hooking a rug or a wall hanging? The answer will determine the type of fabrics, hooking techniques, and composition you will need. A floor rug should be seen from all sides, while wall art is viewed straight on. A wall hanging can be hooked with fancy stitches. A floor rug should be hooked with traditional loops.

Vertical or horizontal. Do you want a dramatic vertical composition, a small square for a delicate theme, or a narrow rectangle? Most artists choose a horizontal shape for landscapes and a vertical shape for portraits. The size and shape of the design will determine the type and size of your rug backing and the width of your fabric strips. Lissa Williamson chose a less common circular shape for *Lighthouses*. This realistic pictorial is a delightful rendition of a popular subject.

Borders. Do you want to include a border? This decision is a personal one.

COMPUTER SOFTWARE CAN HELP

Adobe Photoshop Elements is a wonderful program that you can install on your computer. It will permit you to edit and enhance your photographs. An entire book can be written about using this program. I use the simple edit button and enhance the color and contrasts of my photographs. In addition, I may convert a photo from color to black-and-white to more easily see the values in my picture.

Note: To convert a photo from color to black-and-white—choose "Full Edit." At the top in the tool bar choose "Enhance." Lots of options will appear in the window. Scroll down to "Convert to Black and White" and press OK. Your color photograph will instantly become a black-and-white photograph. Save this image and print.

In the past I have eliminated borders in my pictorial rugs thinking they distracted from my focal point, but over time I find myself reconsidering and adding them frequently to frame my work. I believe in keeping them simple. If you choose a border, keep the following points in mind:

- Always include colors from the center of the rug in the border.
- Darker colors are better along the outer edge of a rug, especially if it is intended for the floor; dark colors weigh more visually and will anchor the piece.
- Determine the width of your border. The wider the space, the more attention is drawn to this area. A common width is 5" to 10". Consider four borders of unequal width in a wall hanging for an abstract approach.
- Separate the border from the center with a line of straight hooking in a contrasting color.
- Use the border to continue telling the story by adding a place, a person's name, or a line of relevant verse.
- Scrolls and flowers are among the endless possibilities to be included.
- Leave a few inches between your interior and the border.
- Let the theme of your rug spill over the border. This technique is called breaking the border.
- If you are in doubt about including a border, leave enough space for it and decide later.

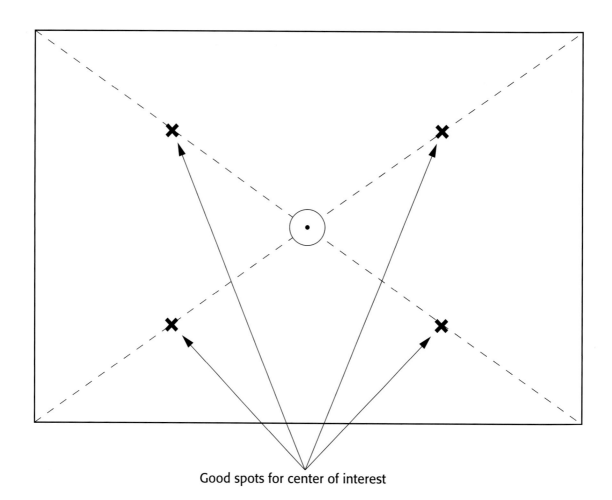

Good spots for center of interest

Correct placement for the center of interest. Ink on paper. Drawing by Jane Halliwell Green, Edgewater, Maryland, 2008.

Principles of design checklist

If you are drawing your own design keep these points in mind. If instead you have a preprinted pattern, you still have control over many of these principles. It is usually acceptable to the designer if you move things around a bit and add embellishments.

Center of interest

Every piece of art needs to have a focal point, or one area that is the star of the show. Every choice you make in your design leads the viewer to look at this place. This focal point is also referred to as the impact area or center of interest. What will your center of interest be? It can be anything you choose it to be. If you are working on a landscape, avoid committing too much space to the sky or ground because they can compete with your center of interest. An exception might be a design where the sky is intended to be the focal point.

Artists often take the least obvious object in a composition and give it the most important role. For instance, instead of making a lighthouse in a maritime scene the center of interest, choose the rocks in the foreground instead. A viewfinder can assist you in choosing the right focal point. A small 4 x 6 mat purchased in a local art store can serve as a viewfinder. If you look through the 4 x 6 mat, you can capture parts of a landscape in the opening and make some decisions about your composition, including the placement of key subjects.

Do not place the center of interest in the dead center of your picture. Place the focal point to the right or left of center and commit the greatest amount of space to it. The easiest way to determine its location is to find the center of the pattern. Draw two diagonal lines intersecting this center. Find the halfway point on each diagonal section. You will have four good areas in which to establish the focal

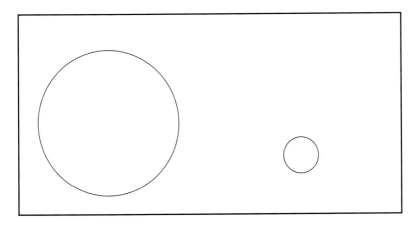

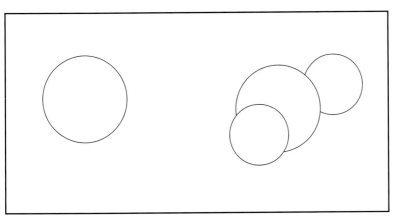

No balance above—better balance below. Ink on paper. Drawing by Jane Halliwell Green, Edgewater, Maryland, 2008.

point. In most rug designs, the center of interest falls in the midground area. Your center of interest should be lighter than its surroundings and visually interesting.

Shape

Include a variety of shapes. Every shape should be interesting. Group objects artistically and do not spread them evenly apart in perfect horizontal rows. Think in odd numbers, such as three trees or five houses. Most painters speak of the "division of threes," and prefer a threefold division of space. Vary the number and size of openings in buildings. Repeat similar shapes but make them slightly different. Repeat strong colors in three places also.

Balance

Remember to balance the weight of the objects in the design. A large house on one side of a design needs to be balanced on the other side by a group of objects of similar weight. In fiber we also add

weight to objects with the texture and color of our materials. Textures have more visual weight than smooth fabrics; warm colors are heavier than cool colors, and dark hues add weight.

Visual pathways

A good work of art makes the viewer a participant in it, rather than a mere spectator of it. One purpose of the foreground is to lead the viewer toward the focal point. Make sure the viewer's eye can move easily through your picture. Have an entering point for the eye, usually at the lower left of the composition, but not at the corner or center. Be careful of roads that exit at the corner—pull them a few inches toward the interior of the picture plane; off-center points of entry make a more interesting composition.

Touch the borders in three places. This can be as simple as a tree branch that touches the border on one side and a shadow that connects with the opposite

Reunion on Quince Street, 38" x 25", #2- and 3-cut wool on linen. Designed and hooked by Lynne Fowler, Oranock, Virginia, 2007.

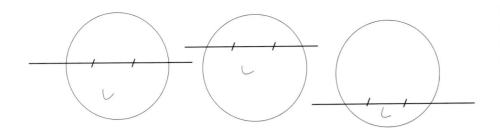

Placement of the horizon line. Ink on paper. Drawing by Jane Halliwell Green, Edgewater, Maryland, 2008.

edge. These connections tie the design to the picture plane and give it additional weight.

Include diagonal lines and shapes in your design, as they provide a greater sense of movement than do vertical and horizontal lines.

Avoid relentless detail.

Perspective

You don't have to be an expert on perspective, but understanding it will make your picture believable. Perspective emerged in Italian art in the 15th century. Before that time, pictures were flat. Perspective creates the illusion of depth. If you are hooking a primitive piece, don't worry about perspective. Objects are allowed to float through space and be any size that you choose. Our ancestors did not worry about perspective—they drew and hooked their environment as they experienced it. Their rugs certainly have a childlike quality that demands an adult value when appraised by experts.

Lynne Fowler designed and hooked *Reunion on Quince Street*. Lynne and her college friends get together every three years to relive old memories and this rug tells that story. The perspective in this piece—the narrowing of the road and the perfect slant of the brick buildings and windows—is exceptional. Lynne draws us right down this road.

Horizon

In a realistic or impressionistic hooked piece, give your scene the impression of depth by first locating the horizon, which is the line at eye level. Do not draw the horizon line through the center—this divides your composition in half. A better placement is one-third of the way down from the top or one-third of the way up from the bottom. The easiest horizon to see is the one where sky meets water. If your picture is a landscape and you place the horizon line low, you are giving importance to the sky. On the other hand, if you place it high, the land becomes more important. Think of the horizon line as an imaginary line that changes depending where you are looking. If you roll your eyes back in your head to look up at the ceiling, the horizon shifts up. The horizon is always drawn parallel to the horizontal edges of the picture, and it is straight.

Objects in recession and the vanishing point (VP). Color pencil on paper. Drawing by Jane Halliwell Green, Edgewater, Maryland, 2008.

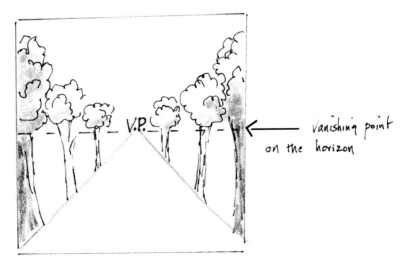

Your goal is to make all the elements in your picture recede into space in the right proportions. Objects above the horizon taper down to this point; objects below it taper upward. As your eye moves toward the horizon and the vanishing point, objects become smaller. You can have multiple vanishing points in a picture.

Key points

- Don't place water, roads, or railroad tracks above the horizon line, or they will appear to stand up—like a wall.
- Reduce the size of your objects as they progress from front to back.
- Consider overlapping objects.
- Downplay objects that rest behind key elements.
- Strive to get the most important subjects in the picture drawn correctly.

This information is important when drawing a building or adjusting the design of a preprinted pattern: all horizontal lines moving away from you that are above eye level are drawn with a downward slant. All horizontal lines moving away from you that are below your eye level are drawn going up. I use a ruler to make sure that the pitch of the roof, windows, and doors on a building are moving toward the vanishing point at the same angle. Practice will make you adept at this. One good drawing class can be valuable also.

Creating depth with values and color

We use perspective to fool the eye into thinking that some parts of the picture are closer than other parts. In addition, values are employed to bring attention to the foreground and take attention away from the background. Controlling values is crucial in a pictorial and almost surpasses everything else in importance.

Each rug must incorporate a good selection of light, medium, and dark values. A common pitfall is producing a rug that becomes lost in the midtones. Consider this: what value do we use up first? The answer, of course, is the middle one. A good rule is to have 50 percent mid-tones, 25 percent light, and 25 percent dark. The focal point is the place to start determining your values. The strongest contrasts are there and everything else is weaker in comparison.

To translate value into color, think in terms of black and white. Consider converting a photo into black and white as discussed earlier. Create a foreground with lots of detail, a middle ground with some detail, and a background with just a suggestion of what is there. Let's look at the three main areas of our picture plane:

- The foreground is bold. Use lots of materials and values. Color can be intense and lead the viewer to the focal point, which is frequently set back from the front, close to the start of the midground. Use warm and bright colors. Remember that warm colors advance and cool colors recede. My rule here is to use 5 to 10 types of materials, including spots, abrashed solids, and tweeds.
- The middle ground can be tricky. You should begin to eliminate some detail and add cool hues but keep a few warm and bright colors. Continue to mix materials and values in the middle ground, but use fewer of them. My unofficial rule is to decrease the variety of colors and materials to three or four selections.
- The background is dull with an emphasis on cool colors like blue and violet. Controlling values in the background is tricky. You need to use more than a single value here or this section will appear to go upward rather than backward. Choose two or three shades emphasizing dull light and medium values with an occasional dark to anchor any element to the back of the picture plane. Use a limited number of materials here—one or two should suffice. The background is only a supporting member of the cast, not the star.

Colors that cool as they recede and diminishing contrasts of light and dark in the background will lend perspective to your piece. To this mix, add objects that grow smaller and overlap each other as they move toward the horizon, and you will successfully trick the eye into seeing depth on a flat surface.

Shadows

Effective shadows can help you create dimension and bring life to your pictorial scenes. They define light and form and add the illusion of reality, making your work more interesting. Shadows occur on the unlit side of an object: a cast shadow occurs when an object interrupts the path of light. Shadows are transparent, not solid. In a realistic piece you have to have them! In the other styles, shadows are a matter of artistic and personal taste.

Shadows are an important consideration in your design for four reasons:

1. Shadows are shapes and add interest to the overall design.

2. Shadows help anchor the entire object on the picture plane and keep it solidly connected to the ground.

3. Shadows add color and contrasts within light areas.

4. Shadows act as bands connecting objects with each other and also with the edges of the picture.

Be observant and look for shadows. Even if you do not get them right the first time, keep working at it. They add a charm and sophistication to your finished product.

When you take reference photos, try to do it early in the morning or late in the day when you'll capture the strongest shadows. Also, keep in mind that the brighter the day, the deeper the shadows. In places like Greece, you'll see spectacular shadows at midday. More frequently midday provides only paler shadows because of the glare reflected from the surfaces around them. These shadows are also shorter because the sun is overhead.

Shadows are rarely gray or black. Instead they lean toward violet, blue, or green. Black is acceptable only in night scenes. Shadows are colored by both the surfaces upon which they fall and the reflection of nearby objects. Look carefully at a shadow's shape. Choose the right blue or purple—stay away from bright hues. You might have to rip out your loops a few times. Light shadows are never white!

A shadow is darker near the base of the object and becomes paler and softer as it moves away from the object. In addition, the intensity of the color decreases with distance. Keep in mind the following, which has always helped me control the values of a shadow: "Everything in the light is lighter than white in shadow. Everything in the dark is darker than white in shadow."

Hooking a shadow with hard edges is easier in rug hooking because the shadow ends abruptly. A diffused shadow requires careful fingering between the shadow color and the sunlit areas. Use a #3 cut to make this happen.

DESIGNING YOUR OWN PICTORIAL

I designed many of my own rugs before I had any formal art training. If you are uncomfortable attempting an original design, trace. Do not copy anyone else's design, but you can take multiple objects and assemble them in a composition and draw the connecting elements yourself. Many readily available resources offer free designs. Dover Publications is one example.

Once you have chosen the shape and size of your rug backing and have a rough sketch of what you are trying to create, make cardboard templates of the pattern's essential motifs. Rearrange these templates until you find a pleasing composition based on the information in this chapter. If an object is too large, trim it with your scissors.

Once you have a satisfactory arrangement, trace these shapes directly on to the rug backing. Add details such as windows, trees, and roads freehand. It often takes a few days to finish this process. I like to arrange the templates in a variety of ways and study them before committing to a final design. You can do it!

CHAPTER 2

Color and Materials

An empty piece of rug backing with a new design drawn onto it is exciting and intimidating at the same time. The real fun starts as you contemplate your project's materials and plan your colors. The color planning of a pictorial design, especially a realistic one, can be a tremendous challenge considering the quantity of materials required and the complexity of multiple backgrounds such as sky, water, and ground.

COLLECTING WOOL

Before you reach this point, be sure you have collected an interesting assortment of wool and other suitable fabrics. No one can say this style of rug hooking is boring, and those of us who have done repetitive designs appreciate this quality.

You will use lots of materials in your pictorial rug, so a bag of scrap material is handy. Start a collection by visiting your local thrift shop and learn how to disassemble woolen garments. Your choice of materials depends on two major factors: 1) will your fiber art be mounted on the wall or the floor, and 2) do you intend to hook with fine strips (#3 and #4) or wider ones (#6, #7, or #8). Any material that can be cut and pulled up into a loop is acceptable for a wall hanging, including unspun wool, embroidery floss, and fancy yarns. The best choice of fabric for floor coverings is 100 percent wool or rug yarn because of its durability.

Seek out flannel-weight woolen fabric. Purchase skirts, shirts, and pants, but avoid jackets and coats as they are difficult to disassemble and yield little material in return for great effort. Blanket-weight wool is too heavy, and men's suit material, even if marked 100 percent wool, is too light. Look for the 100 percent wool label, or second best, Pendleton, Evan Picone, Nordstrom's, or one of the better clothing manufacturer's labels. If the fabric contains some man-made materials and you love the pattern, go ahead and purchase it with the understanding that it could be difficult to hook and may have to be cut wide. Anything marked 20 percent wool and 80 percent acrylic should be avoided. You can use poorer quality remnants in the small spaces of your rug but not in large background areas.

Be on the lookout for green plaids, small tweeds of all colors (especially black and whites), and lots of gray in the lighter shades. You can never have enough textured wool for pictorials.

Durability is not necessary in a wall hanging, so any material that can be pulled up into a loop is acceptable. Raffia can be hooked, and you may find a place for its inclusion. Velveteen frays a bit when hooked, but it makes soft plush grass. T-shirts are an inexpensive option—you might consider dressing a figure in a red T-shirt hooked with the real thing. Yarn has always been popular. Thick rug yarn is easier to handle, but some of the new skeins such as eyelash yarn can provide fabulous effects. I like to include eyelash yarn in my bird nests. Try boucle for wonderful texture, especially in foliage. It will be easier to hook if you work with a double strand. If the yarn is thin, it may be better to leave the tails below the surface. Unspun wool is good for mimicking puffy clouds, mossy trees, and smoke rising from chimneys.

My favorite unusual material is metallic needlepoint yarn or tape. Squeeze it between the loops when a shimmer is required somewhere in the picture. Try it in water or snow for a highlight. Hook it on the handle of an

Yarns and unspun wool, boucles, mohair, eyelash, polyester, and rug yarn.

umbrella or anywhere you need a shine or the look of metal. Metallics are slippery, so they work best when squeezed in last, when the neighboring loops can hold them in place.

CHOOSE A BACKING MATERIAL

When it comes to selecting a backing for a rug, I prefer linen or cotton rug warp. I dislike the spongy feel of monk's cloth and its tendency to stretch. Burlap is not the most durable of backings, so I have stopped using it completely. Making a hooked rug or wall hanging is such a big investment of time, so why not create it with the best materials?

DYEING WOOL

If you are a beginning rug hooker, dyeing your own wool might be overwhelming. Instead purchase already-dyed wool until you have completed a few rugs. A list of wool suppliers is in the resource section.

Before using any of the dye formulas presented in this book, thoroughly soak the wool in water with a capful of a wetting agent so the wool will absorb the dye more readily. A wetting agent insures that the wool will be thoroughly soaked. Synthrapol and liquid laundry detergents are wetting agents. Cushing Perfection acid dyes, PRO Chemical acid dyes, and Majic Carpet dyes are used in these formulas. The Cushing formulas are designated by name alone (such as Canary and Sky Blue); PRO Chemical dyes are designated by both a name and a number (such as #233 Orange and #490 Blue); and Majic Carpet dyes are designated by both name and brand. It is perfectly acceptable to mix all three brands in one dye formula, and I do that often. Each chapter describes how to use each of these formulas in relation to individual pictorial elements.

General dyeing guidelines

■ All the formulas in the book are written for 1 yard of fabric unless otherwise noted.
■ Never boil wool; to do so will cause it to felt. Felting occurs when the wool fibers interlock to form a dense mass and the material shrinks. Felted wool is not acceptable as a hooking material.
■ It takes 20 to 30 minutes at a low simmer to set the color for most formulas. Simmer is achieved when you begin to see bubbles coming up from the bottom of the pot just prior to a boil.
■ Remember that wool always looks darker when it is wet, so keep that fact in mind when considering values.
■ Many of the formulas use the word "abrash." This is an Arabic word commonly used in the Oriental rug industry which means to mottle or streak the wool. To abrash a piece of fabric, pour dye directly on the fabric and then dissipate the spot it makes by pushing the wool under the water. Fabrics with subtle changes of value will result, providing a selection of interesting fabrics. Avoid flat, unabrashed solids in your rugs; pictorials demand varied materials.
■ Each formula is dissolved in 1 cup very hot, almost boiling water unless otherwise noted. Heat the water in a microwave, and for extra safety, place a wooden spoon in the microwave-safe cup as you heat it up. The spoon will stop an explosion of the hot water in the cup if the heat gets too high.
■ White vinegar is my mordant of choice. A mordant sets the color and makes your fabric color-fast.
■ Take your time and do not rush. It is important to give the wool time to cook.
■ All of my formulas are done on the stove top in either a large soup pot or a flat, square turkey roaster.

Dye methods

I dye my wool using these four common dyeing methods.

Over dyeing

Almost every piece of wool in a pictorial is dyed. Wool right off the bolt and flat colors found in the local thrift shop need to be over dyed before being used in your pictorial. You may choose one dye to tone down a piece of fabric or instead choose to "marry" a group of different

Over-dyed plaid, before and after.

fabrics by forcing color out of the wool with detergent and putting it back into the material with vinegar.

Plaids that contain lots of white areas must be over dyed. The photograph above shows before and after examples of a blue-and-white plaid over dyed with blue. The over-dyed plaid could be included in a water scene. The untouched piece would stand out instead of blend in.

Rug hookers often have trouble deciding what color to use in over dyeing a plaid. When in doubt, always choose one of the colors present in the plaid and you will be making a safe choice.

Spot dyes

Spot dyes are done with two to five solutions. Each solution is dissolved in 1 cup boiling water.

Start by tightly squeezing and scrunching the material in a turkey roaster. Spot the fabric like a checkerboard using all of your dye solutions. Pour approximately 2 cups water with about $^1/_3$ cup vinegar in the pan either on top or under the wool. If you pour the water-and-vinegar solution under the wool, the fabric will come up spottier; pour it on top and it will be less spotty. The more water added to the pan,

the less prominent the spots will be. Simmer 20 to 30 minutes until all of the dye has been taken up by the wool.

Jar dyeing

Jar dyeing is a good way to make six values of color. Use large 1-quart canning jars. Avoid using large mayonnaise or other food jars because they break easily. Dissolve all dyes in 1 cup boiling water. Place the jars in a roasting pan filled halfway with water. Also fill each of the jars halfway to two-thirds full of water. Add dye solution to the jars following this value chart:

> **Value 1:** $^1/_4$ tsp.
> **Value 2:** $^1/_2$ tsp.
> **Value 3:** 1 tsp.
> **Value 4:** $1^1/_2$ tsp.
> **Value 5:** 1 Tbsp.
> **Value 6:** 2 Tbsp.

Place a 6" x 12" piece of wool in each jar. Stir the wool in the jars well and bring the water in the pan to a simmer. The water in the jars will be very hot also. After 20 minutes, add 1 tablespoon of white vinegar to each jar. Let the wool cook and stir it frequently until the wool absorbs all the color of the dye solution and the water in the jars is clear. Rinse the wool and allow it to dry. This same procedure can be done in open stock pots if you have larger pieces of wool to dye.

Dip dyes

A dip dye is created when multiple colors are placed on the same strip of wool by dipping the wool into one or more simmering dye pots.

As a rule, I measure my strip to be four times longer than the length of the object being hooked. If I am doing a simple dipped piece with only one color, I use one dye pot. An example of this is one piece of wool dipped in a color that will be dark on one end and light on the other. The first part of the strip is darker, but as the wool grabs the color the dye disappears from the dye pot. When I dip the last half of the strip, since most of the

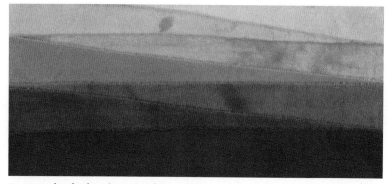

An example of values in an 8-value swatch.

color is gone, the opposite side of the strip will be lighter. When I have two colors on one strip of fabric, I use two pans. The dyes and vinegar are placed in the pans *at the same time*.

Wear heavy plastic gloves when you dip. Dip half of the wool strip in one pan for approximately 3 to 4 minutes. Now dip the other half of the strip for 3 to 4 minutes, allowing the colors to merge in the center. Always keep the wool moving so that harsh lines do not form on the fabric. Because dip dyeing is accomplished quickly, you will need a third pan filled with clear water and vinegar to simmer the dips for about 20 minutes after you have applied the colors. This final step sets the color.

> **Tip:** *When dipping skies make sure the selvage is at the top of the wool and don't try to handle more than a half yard at a time. The strongest piece of wool is cut parallel to the selvage. The top of the sky is next to the selvage, and the horizon level is on the bottom side.*

A few dye tricks

Wool can be simmered in a dye bath with $1/2$ cup laundry detergent to release its color. This method works particularly well with recycled fabrics and what we refer to as "bleeders." The color seeps out fast, and if you add a variety of materials to the pot, they will pick up the color. After 30 minutes, add white vinegar to force the color back into the fabrics. You'll end up with lots of interesting pieces for rocks, water, and foliage to name only a few.

One of my favorite tricks is to take strips of this garish wool (such as orange, turquoise, and hot pink) that I would never use directly in my art and pin them together, alternating white wool with color. I place three strips on the floor and loosely braid them together. I push these braided strips into my dye pot. Then I follow the same directions to bleed out and add back color. Both methods result in an array of interesting fabrics.

Another trick is to cut open the empty dye packages you receive from Cushing. Place a layer of these opened dye packages on presoaked wool. There is always some dye residue within these seemingly empty packages. Place the wool and the packages in a flat pan with a small amount water, add $1/4$ cup vinegar, and simmer for 30 minutes. Pick off the packages and wash the wool when you are finished, and you will be left with an interesting batch of materials.

Clean your spoons in a jar of table salt after measuring each formula. When the jar of salt gets dirty, pour some of this salt on presoaked wool with a little vinegar and simmering water. This trick will give you some very unusual grays with tiny pin pricks of color. I have used material dyed in this fashion to hook sand.

By now you will realize that it is rare to use any material in a pictorial that has not been touched in some way by a trip to the dye pot. The goal is to create a large number of interesting and related pieces of fabric. Sometimes a particular element will turn out sensational simply based on selecting the perfect fabric.

COLOR AND MOOD

Color can enhance or destroy a piece of hooked art. Like all styles of rug hooking, color should be balanced and repeated. More than anything else, however, color sets the mood in the pictorial rug. Some artists strive to match the local color; others don't want to be literal and instead use color to express feelings or mood. A decision one way or another will be based on an individual's preferences and will result in a piece that reflects the artist's style.

Cool colors are melancholy and recede; warm colors are cheerful and advance. The color of the sky is the big mood setter in a pictorial, so it must be carefully planned at the dyeing stage. In the chapters that follow I'll present dye formulas for specific design elements such as sunset skies, stone walls, autumn trees, and more. But for now, let's look at some common colors and how they affect a pictorial rug.

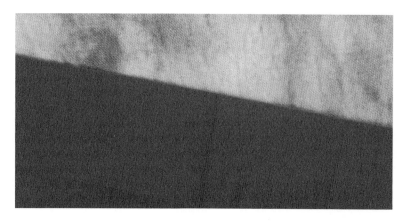

Greens: good and bad choices.

same piece hooked into your rug. It is better to dye a lighter value of gray (with $1/32$ tsp. Cushing's Silver Gray over $1/4$ yard white or natural wool) than to try to get by with something off the shelf.

Black

Black is the absence of light and should only be used in limited quantities. I prefer anything over basic black. When black is required, I choose dark gray or antique black instead. Make a quick antique black by over dyeing 1 yard dark green wool with $1/4$ tsp. black dye dissolved in 1 cup hot water. Another alternative is to over dye a variety of darker recycled wools, bleeding out some of the color and adding black dye and vinegar to pull some color back in.

White

White has greater visual strength than other values. It has a spotlight quality. I prefer white that has been toned down with a tiny bit of Cushing's Taupe, Ecru, Old Ivory, Champagne, or Silver Gray. Over-dyed white wool will still look white in a pictorial if it contrasts with the materials surrounding it. Avoid bright white fences and snow. Balance the spots of white carefully, keeping in mind that they draw attention.

Based on these suggestions, you can see that avoiding most vividly bright colors and materials in your pictorials is ideal. Do something to tone them down: take color out, over dye with the complement to "gray" the color, or over dye pastel wool such as beige and pink.

Spot-dyed materials work best in primitive pieces. Use them judiciously in realistic designs, as they can be too busy. Combining them with abrashed solids and tweeds is a better approach. When I go to the dye pot to prepare spot formulas for my pictorials, I blend the colors well by using more water in the pan and pushing the wool completely under the water.

Complements

Two colors directly opposite each other on the color wheel are complements.

Green

People in general have too many preconceived ideas about color—skies should be blue, clouds white, grass green, and so forth. These ideas are not always accurate. For example, a green area in a pictorial rug can, and should, run the gamut from blue-green to gray-green to yellow-green and shades of blue and violet.

I do many landscape pictorials, and I always use large quantities of green, but a pictorial can be overpowered by green. I challenge both myself and you to find acceptable alternatives. Grass in the distance can be blue, and grass in the shadows can be violet. Bushes can be red, gold, blue, and brown. Include an abundant variety of texture and value and, more importantly, lean to the light side of your hues. Do not get stuck with the endless green meadow, which can happen easily if you don't think beyond the common choices.

Gray

Gray is a chameleon. It absorbs the colors around it and will appear as the complement of the color beside it. Therefore, a neutral gray next to a yellow may appear to have a lavender tint; next to red, it may appear to be green. Gray is available in many values and can be used effectively in creating light and dark areas in your picture. Most pictorials need very light gray. Darker shades of gray can be overused and lighter shades are hard to find, so we often reach into our wool stash and grab the medium values hoping they will work. Gray material held in the palm of your hand looks lighter than the

Some examples are blue and orange, purple and yellow, and green and red. Together in the dye pot, they will "gray" each other. Hooked side by side in a rug, they grab the eye. A good location for these pairings in a rug is around its center of interest.

HOOKING TECHNIQUE

Now it is time to think about hooking technique. The rest of this book goes into detail about specific design elements, but this section offers some general advice about how to hook pictorials.

First, pull out your visual aids and keep them within reach. A cookbook holder can be used to prop up a visual aid so you can see it easily. Determine from which direction the light is coming—right, left, or front. Make a decision and be consistent with it, and shadows will be easy to place (see the section on shadows in chapter 1). Draw a sun and an arrow on your pattern to remind yourself of your choice. Don't be afraid to provide yourself with a written road map.

Season and time of day

In some pictorial landscapes, the sky is the background. Choose this design scheme carefully as it sets the mood for your entire rug. If your design lacks a sky, your first decision will be whether you want a light or a dark background. A fair amount of contrast should exist between the design elements and the background. If you choose the background color first, it will help direct the rest of your color planning. For the elements or objects surrounded by the background, lay a selection of color choices on top of the background fabric to see how they work together. It is easy to get frustrated here, so have confidence and carry on.

Focal point first

Hook the center of interest first, which is often in the foreground or toward the midground and less frequently in the background. This hooked area sets the stage for the entire piece. Work outward from the center of interest. Once you establish the strength of your color and materials at the focal point, every other element will be slightly toned down in comparison. Think of the focal point as your benchmark.

Simplify the hooking process by working on one section at a time. It is easy to be overwhelmed by the immense amount of detail. Divide the space in your mind and think of it as a group of small scenes.

Flow of the design

The direction of your hooking helps define the shapes of your design elements. Most lines flow in an obvious direction. For example, tree trunks flow vertically and skies horizontally. Consider the force of gravity and the weight of the objects when determining the flow of your design. If you can, avoid outlining and filling an area unless you are working on a primitive design.

Each object in your picture must have a shadow at its base to anchor it. I like to define this technique as "grounding." If an object is not grounded, it will appear to float off the surface of the design. I will explain how to ground specific objects in later chapters.

Hook on or just inside the pattern line for tiny pictures or they will expand dramatically. Do not attempt to pack too many loops in a small area.

Special effects

I believe in using whatever method works to create special effects—even if it means breaking some established rules and protocol. Here is a summary of my favorite special effects. (More details will be forthcoming in the chapters that follow.)

■ Cut it wide and hook it low. One example of this technique is the rug hooker who is doing a fine cut (#3 or #4) project who would like to include a piece of fabric that is of poor quality. It is acceptable to cut the poorer quality fabric wide (a #8 cut, for example) and include it with the smaller loops, provided the height of all the loops remains the same.

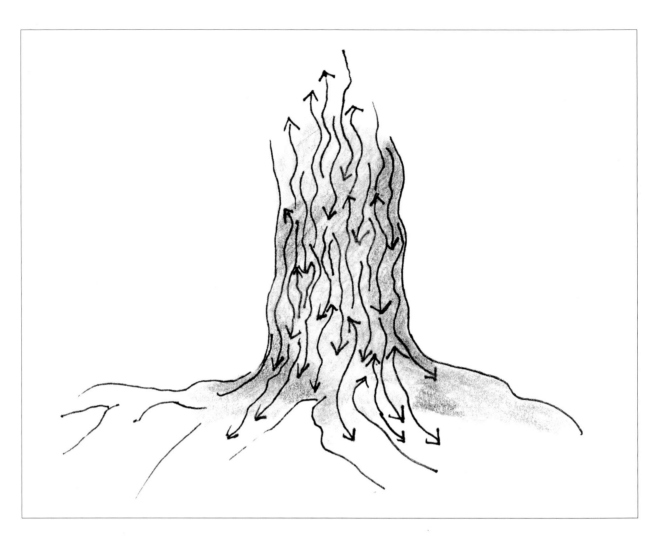

Fingering and staggering tails in a tree trunk. Ink on paper. Drawing by Jane Halliwell Green, Edgewater, Maryland, 2008.

■ Pixelating. This technique is a personal favorite. When hooking foliage of any kind, twist two or three loops into packets and spread the packets over an area to create a textured surface. Details on this technique can be read in the chapter on trees.

■ Meandering. Normal hooking done around the pixelating technique.

■ Skipping values. We are taught not to skip values (or shades), but sometimes it is necessary in order to create contrasting areas.

■ Crossovers. You will find some crossovers on the back of my pictorials. I use this technique when the hooking area is tiny. For example, I may be hooking a sky, and rather than cut a tail every time I come to a tree branch, I'll carry the tails over the existing hooking. This action leaves crossovers on the back of the rug.

■ Shagging. Instead of flat hooking, raise your loops up higher than you normally would and then cut them off. This trick is great for hooking grass.

■ Shagging the border. Execute one narrow line of shagging between flat hooking all around the border. It catches the viewer's eye!

■ Loop shagging. Pull the loops up higher than the normal height and leave them that way. This technique is very effective as a flower center.

■ Reverse hooking. Pull out loops and rehook an area. It's an advantage rug hookers have over painters. When painters make a mistake, the expensive canvas or paper is ruined; we simply rip out our errors and begin again in the same spot. This makes rug hooking very forgiving.

■ Fingering. Stagger the lines of hooking so that the tails are at different intervals. This technique is called fingering because the rows look like the meshed fingers of two hands. It is useful in all styles of rug hooking and will make the transition between various materials and values look seamless.

■ Shimmering. Squeeze some iridescent embroidery floss between the loops as a highlight. This is a great technique to use on angel wings and water.

■ Tunneling. This technique can be useful in outlining an area that needs to be emphasized. Place the loops so that they form a tunnel, meaning that the loops are end to end rather than shoulder to shoulder. You should be able to stick your hook through the opening of the tunnel and pass through it.

■ Sculpting. Often associated with the Waldoboro rugs of Maine, this technique requires hooking loops high and filling as many holes in the foundation as possible for dense coverage. After hooking, remove the piece from the frame and clip all the loops. The sculpted area is raised above the height of the normal loops. This visually interesting technique is ideal for clouds, hills, birds, and bushes.

■ Bundling. Flat hooking in irregular circular or scalloped shapes is a great way to use up scraps of wool.

■ Beading. Sometimes it helps to twist two differently colored strips under the backing so you can pick up a loop of one color and a loop of another without clipping and cutting. This technique was used to hook the flag pole in the *Old Mill on the Eastern Shore* where the red and white stripes alternated with each stitch. This wall hanging is featured as a free design in chapter 12.

■ Unspun wool. To make an element in a pictorial look fluffy, hook it with unspun wool. This technique is perfect for clouds and smoke. Turn your rug over so that the back of the rug is facing you and hook from this side. The fluffy part will end up on the front of your work. This element should be the last thing you hook so you can easily see the shape of the design from the back and have a guide as to where the unspun wool should be placed.

■ Impressionistic cows. Sandwich one white loop between two black loops and you have a cow in the distance.

■ Impressionistic sheep. Hook two or three loops of white and two black tails beneath.

As you hook, remember the advice of every art teacher: what our eyes actually see and what our minds think we see are two different things. Get your mind out of the way and forget what you should hook. Instead, record what you see. In other words, you know the shape of a cow, but when hooking a farm scene, you can hook a few loops to create the overall impression of the animal in the background.

In the next chapters, we will delve into the details of hooking all the elements in pictorial design. Have courage and do the best you can. One of my teachers once said, "Don't let correctness get in the way of expression." I love that sentiment and I will leave you with that thought as you move ahead.

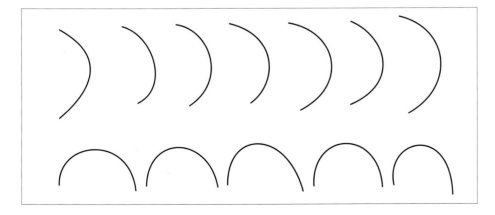

Tunneling and normal loops. Ink on paper. Drawing by Jane Halliwell Green, Edgewater, Maryland, 2008.

CHAPTER 3

Buildings

You cannot say "pictorial rug" without thinking of some sort of building. Before we build our hooked structures, let's review the foundation upon which we place the first board, brick, or stone.

Most buildings, especially historic ones, have quite a bit of charm—and charm brings detail. It is better to let the viewer imagine the individual parts while you create the illusion of a complete structure. Artists who specialize in primitive rugs are experts at illusion because they simplify the piece down to the barest walls and windows and add just enough detail on a house to give it the correct color and character. Don't get pulled in by the little individual parts and lose a sense of the whole. The mood, harmony, and charm are what count in the end. Values—light and dark patterns—and the sense of the story are more important than the details.

For those of you specializing in fine-cut impressionistic pictures, and for the realistic hookers who strive to capture it all, it is important to confine the detail to the impact area and eliminate embellishments in the middle ground and background.

Start by studying the building. Get to know it well. Someday your rug might belong to the historical record for the community. Decide how prominent this structure will be in your picture and place it toward the front, but not smack in the middle of the picture plane as discussed in chapter 1. If your design has multiple structures, think of them as a group of rectangles and triangles representing walls and roofs. Group these shapes together. If you are designing your own structure, draw it as accurately as you can and remember that a straight-on view is easier to draw and hook than a side view.

Vary the number of openings in the structure. If you must have two openings, make one large and one small, one square and one rectangular, one dramatic and one subdued. If the number of openings is large, emphasize some and de-emphasize others.

Finally, for the designers out there, try an unusual interpretation of the scene. Consider imposing floral detail on top of the building as in the wall hanging in chapter 12, *Old Mill on the Eastern Shore*. Change the shape of the backing from the typical landscape or portrait format. Experiment with ovals, circles, and long rectangular shapes.

This rule of thumb applies to all structures: always shadow the underside to connect it to the earth. These types of shadows require a very dark value. Do not underline, but instead use irregular lines of hooking to ground the building within the picture plane. Extend the shadow line beyond the end of the structure.

ROOFS AND CHIMNEYS

Roofs come in many styles—from the typical gray slate you see in subdivisions all over the United States to 19th century mansard roofs with scalloped tiles to the thatched roofs of Ireland and England. Regardless of the roof type, here are some basic guidelines of hooking roofs.

If you plan a dark roof, choose a lighter house color and vice versa. Choose your materials carefully. Soft gray or brown tweed gives the look of shingles without having to hook them individually. Find tweeds with specks of bright color in them, but avoid busy plaids and spot dyes. Roofs are rather unimportant—don't draw too much attention to them.

All textured materials look darker when they are hooked, so choosing the right material is tricky. Scrunch the material up in your fingers to get a better idea of the final results. This process will help you to accurately see the values.

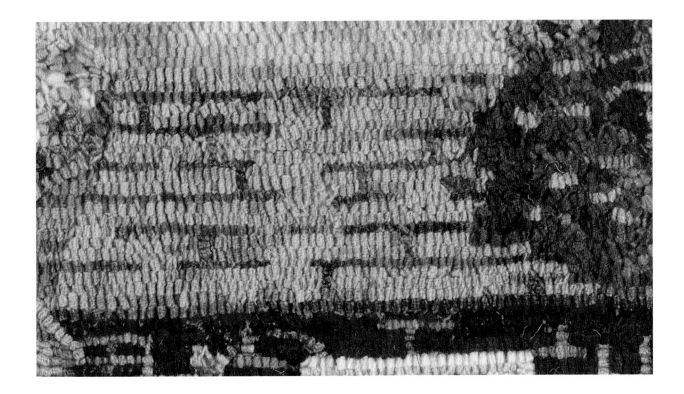

If two roofs connect or touch each other, use two different materials to set them apart from each other.

Grays and tans are common roof colors, but light blue and red are also good choices. Selecting a light blue roof surrounded by fall foliage colors, or a red roof surrounded by green foliage, adds excitement to the picture. These color combinations (red and green, and blue and orange) are complements, or opposites on the color wheel. Complements complete each other and therefore lend extra charm to your work.

Shadow colors are also important. My first choice is blue, followed by purples, grays, and browns. The shadows cast by individual tiles should be hooked in a value deeper than the roof. Avoid the hard look of plain black wool—cast it aside.

When you work with a large variety of recycled wool, you'll end up with less-than-perfect fabric. So the rule is to cut it wide and hook it low. It is perfectly acceptable to combine different cuts in a rug as long as the height of your loops is consistent.

Shingles

Hook the shingle shadows first. It is unnecessary to hook every line. Add a few to imply that more exist. The shadow lines should be compatible with the shingles—dark brown against tan; dark gray or black against gray tweed. Fill between the tiles using straight horizontal lines starting at either the top or bottom. Place a shadow under the eaves near the gutter. For a small roof, use tiny gray, black, or brown tweed and omit the shingle shadows.

Tile

The task here is to keep the curve. Establish the curve first and work up and down from it to fill the scalloped shape. It is very easy for your hooking to become straight. Start with the shadow between the rows of tile. Hook these slightly diagonal lines first. The darkest shadow is at the bottom near the gutter area, and you

Close-up of a shingled roof.

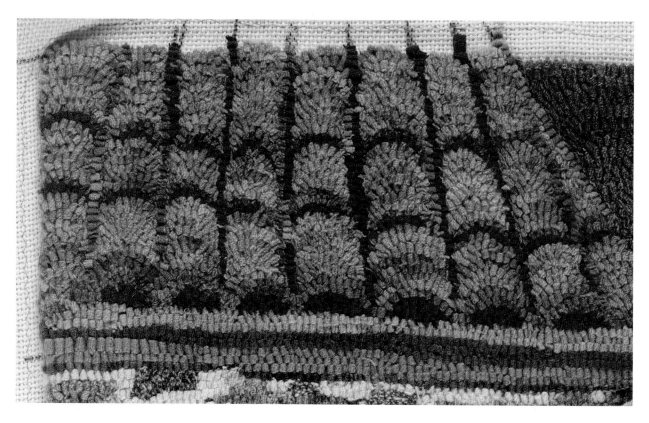

Close-up of a tile roof in *Sorrento Window*, 19" x 13", #3-cut wool on cotton warp cloth. Designed and hooked by Jane Halliwell Green, Edgewater, Maryland, 2008. Hooked as a study piece to illustrate a technique.

may add this next. In *Sorrento Window*, I found a dark brownish red in my scrap bag for the shadow color. For the color of the tiles, I would suggest red-orange with a few loops of moss green for additional realism. I used two values of the dye formula WFS #34 Clay Pot for my tiles (see page 32).

Thatched

Seek a fuzzy look for the thatching. It is worth suffering with a fabric of lesser quality to achieve this effect. The direction of your hooking doesn't matter. Your individual loops should not be prominent when they are hidden in the fluffy materials. You may hook the roof with raffia, but remember it will have to be a wall hanging! You might even try sculpting the roof (trimming the loops so portions of the roof are higher than other parts).

Steeples

Steeples are cone shapes and they will test your hooking skill. Depending on the direction of the light source, part of the steeple is in the light, but as the steeple curves away from the light, it gets progressively darker. As it tapers, it also grows lighter. Keep your light source in mind when hooking other similarly shaped structures, such as windmill towers, silos, and lighthouses.

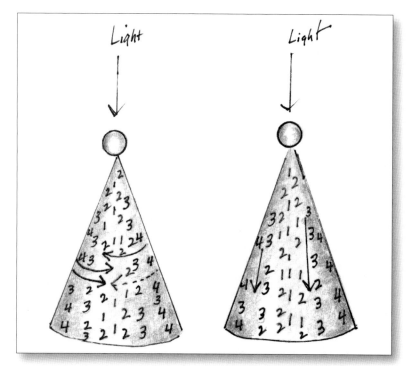

Steeples. Directional hooking vertically and horizontally in Values 1 to 4. Color pencil on paper. Drawing by Jane Halliwell Green, Edgewater, Maryland, 2008.

Hook a steeple in curved horizontal lines if the area is large enough. If the steeple is tiny, you will be forced to hook vertically.

Chimneys

Build a chimney as you work on the roof because they are joined. A shadow under the chimney will cement this connection. A realistic chimney will be light on the side receiving sunlight and dark on the opposite side. Your hooking can be either horizontal or vertical depending on the type of chimney you intend to build.

Hook bricks horizontally between rows of mortar. Hook a concrete chimney vertically. Once the chimney is in place, add smoke rising from it in semicircular lines, making sure the wisps don't disappear into the background.

Gray unspun wool is an excellent choice for smoke if you are making a wall hanging. Hook it into your work from the back side so the wisps of wool will appear on the front side.

POPULAR BUILDINGS
Clapboard buildings

Clapboard houses and churches are not tedious if you suggest the detail instead of hooking every board. Hook the front of the structure and only hint at the detail on the sides. Hook in a horizontal direction. A three- or four-value gradation works well on this type of house. Make a decision regarding the direction of the light source. Hook the lightest side with Value 1 and outline the clapboards with Value 4. Value 2 belongs to the side of the house that is partially shaded, and Value 3 is for the side opposite the light source.

Many clapboard-style homes are white or light colored. Avoid off-the-bolt white wool, which looks chalky and cold. An object in the sunlight will be warm. Notice that the dye formulas for light buildings are generally on the yellow or warm gray side.

Almost any color will work for a house, but avoid green. Pictorials often

Favorite gray swatch for houses of all types.

have an abundance of green trees and bushes, and green can overpower the scene. I prefer blue, red, and yellow houses. Roofs are usually gray, so if I choose a gray house, I choose a beige or brown roof.

Gray House Dye Formula

My favorite white-to-gray house is simply dyed with $1/4$ tsp. #672 Black in 1 cup boiling water. You control the values. Use a piece of wool measuring 18" x 13".

Value 1:
Dip this very light value in a weak solution of Champagne ($1/32$ tsp. in 1 cup water). This will warm up the cold undyed white wool. An alternative to this is not dyeing this piece at all and letting it be the lightest value. I prefer a little tint of yellow.
Value 2: Add 1 tsp.
Value 3: Add 1 Tbsp.
Value 4: Add 2 Tbsp.
Value 5: Add 4 Tbsp.
Value 6: Add 8 Tbsp.

Victorian buildings

Some of America's most beautiful homes were built in the Victorian era, from 1837 to 1901. We are fortunate to have quite a few preprinted patterns of these gorgeous homes. Rug hookers who have taken classes or workshops in Cape May, New Jersey, and Chautauqua, New York—both places known for their outstanding Victorians—are often seen hooking the homes

Stone shapes. Watercolor on paper. Painting by Jane Halliwell Green, Edgewater, Maryland, 2008.

nicknamed "Painted Ladies." Painted Ladies are houses known for the three or more contrasting colors and decorative ruffles and flourishes.

My advice for hooking a Victorian is to use lots of photo references. Your local paint store may even have a book of suggested Victorian colors. Collect the paint chips to use in color planning. Keep your color palette simple, choosing a minimum of three colors for each house. Contrasting colors are necessary to bring out all the ruffles and flourishes in the trim. Common color combinations are pink and peach; green and red; blue and yellow; plum, blue, and white; green, pink, and white; and orange, yellow, and gold. Along with vibrant trim, many Victorians are embellished with colorful stained glass windows, so pull out your strong spot dyes for them.

Stone buildings

The key to a stone building that is the focal point of a picture is to make every stone a different shape and to use a variety of materials. Stones come in multiple variations in shape and color.

How you handle the construction of a stone building depends on its placement in your picture. If the building is in the foreground and prominent, you will want to show a lot of detail in the stone work. If the structure is in the background or in shadow, one piece of textured wool could be enough to transmit the visual message that it is stone. A third choice is to hook two or three stones and suggest that more may be present. If you draw a stone building, be sure to juxtapose the stones so that they fit together like a rough jigsaw puzzle.

Start by hooking the stones. Leave the mortar for last. In an old stone building, vary the shapes as in the illustration. Leave irregular areas around the stones for the mortar. It is OK to fill each individual stone with more than one material. I prefer to hook the interior of my stones with straight lines unless the stone is curved and almost circular. I choose this style because most rocks contain angular or straight lines unless they are greatly worn through abrasion. Do not outline the exterior of the stone and fill it in as you risk ending up with little "basketballs."

Stones are commonly brown or gray, but some have hints of pink, blue, or greenish gold. In combining different materials within the stone follow this rule: use 75 percent of one color plus a touch of a second color. Try browns with a touch of rust, grays with a touch of pink, or beiges with a touch of gray. Tweeds work best for the dominant color.

When the house has medium and dark walls, divide your tweeds into light, medium, and dark values. This can be tricky, but eventually you'll get to know your materials so well that seeing the values will be second nature. In the meantime, hook a small sampler of tweeds side by side and you'll see the values clearly. Every time you find or buy a new piece of textured material, add it to your sampler.

Fill the area around the stones with mortar. Vary the number of lines of mortar to show the irregularity of the building process. Mortar can be too light and jump off the picture, or it can be too dark and disappear into the stones. Off-white, taupe, tan, light to medium gray, and ecru are good color choices. The goal is to see contrast between mortar and stones without drawing attention to this unimportant feature.

In some stone buildings it is unnecessary to add the mortar. In this case, separate your tweed into three piles of light, medium, and dark to create the effect of

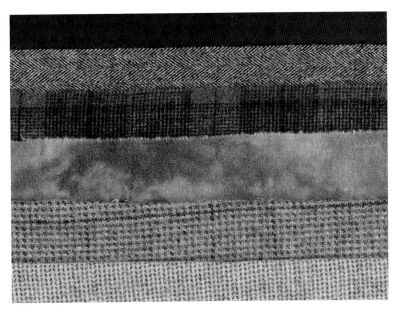

A good selection of materials to use in hooking stones.

light and shadow on the stone. In the front areas, you can outline individual stones for greater detail and leave the receding areas alone.

Roslyn Logsdon, a well-known artist, teacher, and expert in designing pictorial rugs and wall hangings, has traveled throughout Europe and is drawn to mag-

Vaulting 1, York Minster, 19" x 20 ¹/₂", #3-cut wool on linen. Designed and hooked by Roslyn Logsdon, Bethesda, Maryland, 2008.

Staggering bricks. Watercolor on paper. Sketch by Jane Halliwell Green, Edgewater, Maryland, 2008.

nificent stone structures. In *Vaulting 1, York Minster*, on page 29, she has created a Gothic arch. Roslyn comments, "I am so enthralled with the soaring heights and geometric patterning found in the magnificent stone constructions of the 13th and 14th centuries. There is an amazing interplay of light and shadow and repetition of forms and angles. The shadows suggest the hidden depths and create the illusion of space."

Dye Formulas
(Refer to the dye index for formula locations.)
Granite
Stonewall

Brick buildings
Bricks are more regular in shape than stones, but in older buildings, you'll see variation. If your bricks are exactly the same size and shape and you place exactly three rows of mortar around them, then you are hooking a brand-new structure! Add bricks to an existing pattern. It is acceptable to edit and embellish the designer's work from time to time. Draw the shape of your bricks directly on the rug backing. Stagger the bricks as shown in the illustration.

The trick to building believable brick structures lies in the choice of materials. Search for three closely related terra cotta plaids that can be mixed together.

You do not want busy materials. If the appropriate materials are not available, I over dye a small check herringbone or plaid with a red formula. Red plaids that have strong areas of white should be over dyed also.

It might be difficult to divide red plaids into three values. Sometimes it is necessary to go to the dye pot.

In hooking a primitive house, find one good rusty red plaid and outline and fill with the same material. Working with values is not necessary. This also works for a brick structure in the background of your picture.

The trim on a brick house looks sensational in the color blue and its tints. Why? Because blue is the complement of orange.

Dye Formulas
Mortar #1
$1/8$ tsp. Ecru
Dissolve the dye in 1 cup boiling water. Place 1 yard natural wool in a pot of simmering water. Pour the formula directly on the wool, and push and turn the wool. Continue until the formula is gone. Add vinegar and simmer for 20 minutes. If the color is too light, mix another cup of formula and repeat the process.

Mortar #2
$1/8$ tsp. Taupe
Follow the same directions as above.

Over Dye for Bricks #1

Any red plaid or plain red can be over dyed with a green to tone down a bright red. Almost any green will suffice to achieve this effect. I often use $^1/_4$ tsp #728 Green in 1 cup boiling water. I pour the green into the pot and then add the fabric. I add vinegar and simmer until all the color has been taken up by the wool.

Over Dye for Bricks #2

$^1/_{32}$ tsp. #425 Blue

$^1/_8$ tsp. #233 Orange in 1 cup boiling water

PR4 Red Oak

$^1/_2$ tsp. #119 Yellow

$^1/_4$ tsp. #349 Fuchsia

$^1/_{32}$ tsp. #672 Black

Dissolve the three dyes together in 1 cup water. Dye a series of values over natural, beige, yellow, or red plaid wool.

I avoid spot dyes unless they are very subtle. If you are desperate for a very light to medium colored brick, reach for a bit of WFS #34 Clay Pot (see next page).

Stucco and adobe

Stucco and adobe are close cousins of brick. Adobe bricks are cut from clay or yellow river silt and then dried in the sun. They have a rough, crumbly texture and often a dirty yellow or terra cotta color. You can hook these structures with swirling lines, much like filling in a background. The goal is to show character on the exterior.

Materials for stucco and adobe structures.

Nubble Light, 16" x 20", #3 -and 4-cut wool on cotton warp cloth. Karlkraft pattern available through Harry M. Fraser Company. Hooked by Sue Welch, Annapolis, Maryland, 2008.

The light source three ways. Color pencil on paper. Drawing by Jane Halliwell Green, Edgewater, Maryland, 2008.

We do, however, enjoy drawing and hooking them and hope they will be around as historical markers for many centuries.

Each lighthouse has its own special personality, but as a general rule, they all consist of a tower topped by a glassed-in lantern room at the top. Many are surrounded by other buildings including the light keeper's cottage. Some of the towers are made of stone, others wood. They often look like milk bottles, but some like Long Point Light in Provincetown Harbor, Cape Cod, Massachusetts, are square. We consider these structures part of our history. Most of them are now museums.

One of my favorite lighthouses is Nubble Light or Cape Neddick Light, built in 1879. It is the southernmost light in Maine, and it is situated on a barren rock island called the Nubble. My class loved this Karlkraft pattern available through Harry M. Fraser Company. I have included a few versions (page 33, 34, 64).

If you're hooking a lighthouse, you must decide which direction to hook. If the tower is wide enough, you can hook it with curved horizontal lines, changing values as the light dictates. It is easier, however, to hook vertically for ease in changing values. Determine the direction of the light and hook light to dark. The goal is to make a

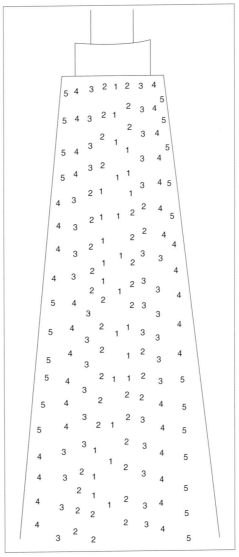

Placement of values: lightest (#1) to darkest (#4) in a lighthouse tower. Color pencil on paper. Drawing by Jane Halliwell Green, Edgewater, Maryland, 2008.

round tower curve. Accomplish this task by carefully working with three to five values. As you work with your palette, you must finger the values together in order to avoid a striped look.

The basic gray formula described on page 27 is a good material for white lighthouse.

WEATHERED WOOD

Barns and bridges are everywhere in the American landscape. Use them as a focal point if they are in the foreground. Similar materials and techniques are used to hook both structures.

Barns

The barn is the heart of a farm, and in a pictorial rug, it is frequently the center of interest. Barns can be built of stones or rest on a stone foundation, but most people will picture the structure as a wooden one. Barns come in all colors, but red is certainly the most familiar. Red absorbs the sun's rays, keeping the building warm. For this reason, barns in northern states are red. In the south, famers use lighter colors to reflect the sun and maintain cooler temperatures in the building.

Silos are built with steel, concrete, or brick and resemble a rocket. Light gray materials are good choices for depicting these structures.

Barns often have large open doors. Fill the hayloft with a gold spot dye. There is no reflective surface to consider here, only the depth of the interior. Hook this interior with a dark gray or dark brown. A second door—often larger than the hayloft—is handled exactly like the opening of a covered bridge. Use two or three values as you hook from light to dark.

Hook the siding on a barn in vertical or horizontal lines. When in doubt regarding the direction of your hooking, choose vertical. Sometimes the decision is based on the proximity of another building. Because barns are often connected to smaller storage buildings, a look of separation is possible by hooking one structure vertically and the other horizontally.

If the barn has a stone foundation, hook the stones first.

For a red barn, choose recycled reds and over dye them with green. Reds can be mixed with brown tweeds and over-dyed plaids in the structure. Pick subtle gray and brown tweeds and abrashed materials for weathered wood. Be careful with plaids as they can be too busy. Many spot dyes are too busy also.

> **Tip:** Any spot dye can be made less busy by using lots of water in the pan. Divide similar textured materials into three piles of similar values and randomly mix and finger them as you hook. It is harder to be constantly changing fabrics in this mixing process, but it is important to do so to avoid the striped look that may result if you do not.

Dye Formula
WFC-3 Barn Red
$^1/_8$ tsp. #338 Red
$^1/_8$ tsp. #502 Brown
$^1/_{32}$ tsp. #725 Green
$^1/_8$ tsp. #233 Orange
Dissolve all the dyes in 1 cup boiling water and add $^1/_2$ cup vinegar to the dye pot. Pour half of the formula into the dye pot and add $^1/_2$ yard white or natural wool. Once the dye is absorbed, pour the remaining solution on the wool to mottle it.

Covered bridges

Covered bridges almost always have succumbed to the weather by changing color and becoming duller and grayer over the years. The interior of the structure should progress from light at the entrance to dark farther inside. To achieve this effect, you need at least two or three values. The direction of the light is important here. One side of the entrance could be a little lighter. The inside is darker than the exterior, and as you move farther into the bridge, the values become darker. I have resorted to using black to achieve this effect.

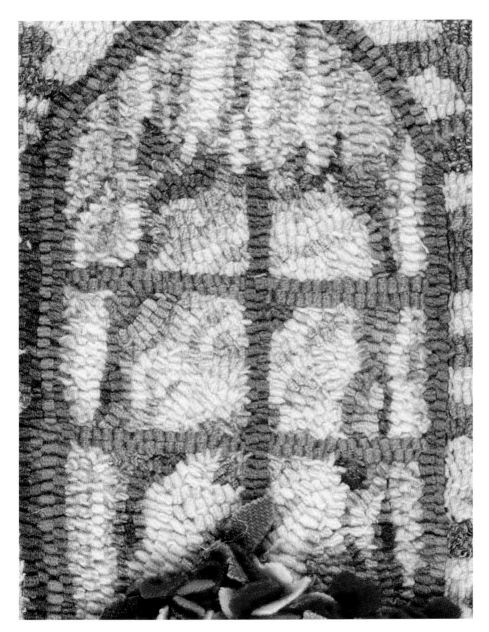

Close-up of window panes in *Sorrento Window*, 19" x13", #3-cut wool on cotton warp cloth. Designed and hooked by Jane Halliwell Green, Edgewater, Maryland, 2008. Hooked as a study piece to illustrate a technique.

A window on the side might look out toward the landscape or in toward the interior of the bridge. Fill it either with landscape greens and blues or with the interior color of the bridge.

If the bridge spans the water be sure to add a shadow underneath in some dark grays or blues.

Always hook the sides vertically on a bridge. Hook the dark accents first, and then the siding in various widths to show wear and tear. The fissures, cracks, and shadows between the boards can be hooked with a narrow strip (#3 or #4) of wool a value or two darker. As with barns, bridges often rest on stone foundations, too, so hook the stones first.

Choose subtle gray and brown tweeds and abrashed materials for weathered wood. Be careful with plaids as they can be too busy. Many spot dyes are too busy also. Use the spot dye information on page 18 to tone down a busy piece of wool.

If a covered bridge is the focal point of your rug, bring color into the picture around the exterior of buildings. This is especially important with covered bridges as the boards are weathered and dull. Surround your bridge with strong purples, blues, and greens.

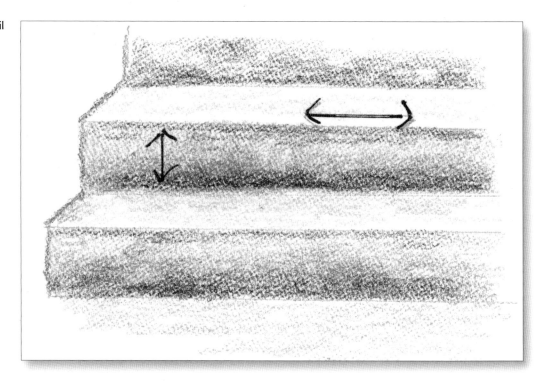

Stairs. Colored pencil on paper. Drawing by Jane Halliwell Green, Edgewater, Maryland, 2008.

TRIM, WINDOWS, DOORS, AND STAIRS

Choose a trim color that is plain and provides a pleasing contrast to the building. Experiment with various values. You want the trim to enhance the structure, not jump out from the picture. The value might be one or two values darker or lighter than the overall color. A white church, for example, could have gray trim; a dark brick building could have a medium brown or gray trim. Think in terms of complementary colors such as blue and rust, purple and gold, or red and green; or select colors side by side on the color wheel, such as blue and purple, gold and brown, or blue and red.

Windows are tricky. They must portray the reflective quality of the glass within them. If you hook the window glass before you add the sky and you don't think it looks right, do not take it out— sometimes you'll have a different opinion once the sky is finished. You can always rip out the glass later. Window glass can easily look like dark holes pasted on the surface or dark buttons that appear to jump off the picture. You can avoid this by choosing the right material in the correct value. People are naturally curious and drawn to openings in buildings, so make the interiors of your windows interesting. Keep the following points in mind and your windows will look sensational:

- The mullions are trim, so hook them first. You don't need to hook the entire window frame. Consider leaving an edge undefined and let the viewer mentally fill it in.
- Glass is dull, not dark. It reflects what is outside. Do not hook the glass with black. Since glass reflects what is outside, use some of the colors outside the building. A light spot dye with a variety of soft pastels often works well. Gray can work, but avoid dark gray.
- Dull gold is great filler when the pictorial's setting is in the late afternoon or evening. The gold simulates a light behind the window. Choose your wool carefully, as bright gold and true yellow will be too bold. The right material is most likely in your scrap bag. Look for a dull gold in medium values.
- If the window is large enough, hook its interior loops either diagonally or in wavy lines. Avoid straight lines unless space is an issue.
- Try to avoid crowding the loops within the panes.
- On a light building, it may be necessary to add a dark line on both sides of the

window, implying the presence of a shutter. Between the shutters, add a light spot dye for the glass. Avoid a dark outline around the entire window frame.

■ Use strong multicolored spot dyes with blues and purples for a stained glass window.

Decorated windows

Sometimes windows are so large that the objects behind the panes can be shown in the picture. If you are faced with this challenge, imagine shapes not objects. Don't try to hook a lamp behind the window—instead hook a triangle and a square. Imply that things exist and let the viewer's imagination do the rest.

I like to hang curtains in my windows, especially the standard white tie-back style. The window has to be large enough to accommodate this added detail. Hook the dark, shadowed creases of the fabric first. Your lines must bend: fabric falls in gentle folds. Next hook the curtain, using light materials around the creases. Sometimes I use some plain white in the lightest area.

If you hang lace curtains, put tiny lace holes in with a shadow color. The lace holes can be as small as two tails. A white-and-gray tweed with flecks of color can make an excellent curtain all by itself. Once the curtain is in place, add a shadow between it and the window glass. Cutting the shadow color narrower than the rest of your hooking and tucking it in around the curtain is the best strategy.

A second way to hang a curtain in a wall hanging is to leave a small amount of space unhooked around the perimeter of the window and attach real lace trim by sewing it to your foundation. This method is easy, and the effect is unique.

Dye Formulas
Snow Spot #1 and **Snow Spot #2**
Both of these dyes make a good curtain fabric. (Refer to the dye index for formula locations.)

Field of Flowers
This formula can be found in chapter 4.

Fireworks
Spot over 1 yard white or pink wool. Also great for stained glass!
$1/4$ tsp. Red-violet in 1 cup water
$1/4$ tsp. Blue-violet in 1 cup water
$1/4$ tsp. Blue in 1 cup water

Doors

Doors seem to have personalities of their own. Decide how important the door in your rug will be. If it is part of the focal point, have fun decorating it. Hang a wreath or drape the door with ivy. A red door will call attention to the spot.

Stairs

Stairs usually invite a little reverse hooking because of their difficulty. If you have enough space (and that is always a consideration), hook the treads horizontally and the risers vertically. If the area is small, simply alternate light and medium value wools and hook horizontally. The treads are usually the lightest area of the stair, the risers darker.

CHAPTER 4

Flower and Vegetable Gardens

Flowers are important in our landscapes. Gardens are often the final pieces of color, and they add charm to a pictorial rug or wall hanging. Let's start with an impressionistic flower garden.

FLOWER GARDENS
Techniques

In the majority of pictorial designs, rug hookers try to create the impression of a flower rather than include the intricate details of petals, stamens, and leaves.

Pixelating

I use the pixelating technique to create sensational cottage gardens. The technique is described in detail in chapter 10. Because the hooking is done in little bundles, reminiscent of pixels, or tiny dots, the hooked dots of color create the impression of a whole garden. This technique takes a long time to do, but it is worth the effort as the final result is unique.

Pixelating should be used in wall hangings, not floor rugs. It can be done in any cut, but it works best with strips cut in #3 to #6. This technique is dramatic on a large rug using a #6 cut because a wider strip makes a larger dot and creates a bulkier texture on the surface of the design. Use leftover strips of wool from your scrap bag. Assemble pinks, blues, yellows, whites, lavenders, and greens; include tweeds, plaids, spots, and abrashed wool. Mixing different widths from #3 to #6 is encouraged for variety. Pixelate throughout your garden, and do not forget to add the dirt underneath the flowers.

Baby proddy

Many of you know that proddy rugs are made by prodding or poking strips of fabric through the linen or burlap foundation from the back side of the rug. In pictorial design, I call this a "shaped proddy." The fabric is shaped to resemble a particular flower petal or leaf. If this petal

or leaf is tiny, I refer to it as a "baby proddy." In baby proddy, the shaped pieces of wool resemble miniature versions of flowers, sometimes only $1/2$" to 1" in length. This technique is ideal for wall hangings or other hooked items not used on the floor. It can be time-consuming, but the finished effect is unusual and will stop viewers in their tracks.

The pieces of baby proddy are small and will fray if they are cut from poor quality fabrics, so use good quality wool and avoid recycled materials. A proddy tool is helpful but not necessary. Proddy hooking is easy to do on any rug backing except fine linen. The weave of fine linen is small, making it difficult to force the shaped pieces through the cloth.

Decide on the flower or flowers you wish to place in your pictorial piece. If you are uncomfortable cutting the shapes freehand, you can create a paper template. Cut the wool using the templates as your guide. It is easier to spend some time cutting and stacking shaped proddy pieces before you add them to your picture. Keep the size fairly consistent, but don't worry if one flower is a little smaller or larger than another. Mark a small X on your rug backing where you will place each flower. Cut out the shape of your flower. Make sure the waist is not too narrow as it will break when poked through the rug foundation. The waist is the center of the proddy shape. It is the part that stays underneath the surface of the hooked piece.

Place the proddy shapes in first and then hook the background second, or leave enough space for the proddy piece and add it after hooking the background. I find it easier to proddy last.

Notice that the template has a left side and a right side. With your hook poke one side under the backing and pull up the other side by grabbing the waist with your hook. Sometimes you have to pull hard to get the other side up. Then meander around your proddy shapes with a variety of greens.

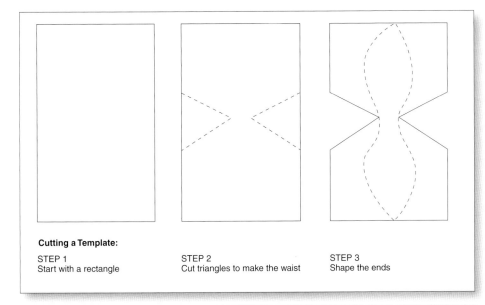

Cutting a template. Ink on paper. Drawing by Jane Halliwell Green, Edgewater, Maryland, 2008.

Cutting a Template:

STEP 1
Start with a rectangle

STEP 2
Cut triangles to make the waist

STEP 3
Shape the ends

Baby proddy templates. Ink on paper. Drawing by Jane Halliwell Green, Edgewater, Maryland, 2008.

SHAPED BABY PRODDY TEMPLATES:

Sunflowers and Daisies

Petunia and Azaleas

Tulip (Large)

Tulip (Small)

Flower (no name)

Cabbage

Leaf #1

Cabbage with "cut ins"

Leaf #2

Corn

Squash Leaf

"Walking the Line"

Sunflowers, hooked and prodded three ways (left to right: #1, #2, and #3), #8-cut wool on linen. Designed and hooked by Jane Halliwell Green, Edgewater, Maryland, 2008.

#4. Close-up of appliquéd sunflower in *Sunflower*, page 110.

Popular Flowers

Tulips

Try prodding a field of tulips. Fill an area with pink, white, and red tulips. Can you imagine how wonderful this would look in a rug inspired by the tulip festivals in Holland? The leaves can be baby proddy shapes. It may be necessary, especially if you have a field of tulips, to tack the pieces down against the backing using matching thread.

Sunflowers and daisies

Everyone loves sunflowers. In a mini-pictorial, try these simple and effective sunflowers.

1. Pixelate the center first using two to three loops of a plaid or check. Then, surround the center with one circle of regular hooked loops. Add a stem and some leaves, and it looks like the real thing. This works best in a #3 to #5 cut. A field of these baby sunflowers is very effective.

> **Tip:** *Stand away from your work or use a demagnifying glass to get a broader view of your picture.*

2. For another impressionistic sunflower, pixelate the center as you did in the first example, but this time pull the surrounding loops up high—about 1/2". I call this "loop shagging." The higher loops will result in a prominent flower that stands out from the picture.

Placement of pixelated roses. Ink on paper. Drawing by Jane Halliwell Green, Edgewater, Maryland, 2008.

3. To make a sunflower a third way, cut five or six petals out of the fabric. Yellow and orange make a wonderful sunflower, and white and gray could be interpreted as a daisy. Hook the center first. Add the background, leaving an area around the center for the prodded shapes. As a final step, poke 5 or 6 petals around the center. Hook a stem and attach the proddy leaves.

4. This fourth sunflower is three-dimensional. Sew a wool appliqué shape on top of the hooking. Leave just enough space to stuff the petal with fiberfill. Sheri De Mate used this creative technique in her rug, *Sunflower*. The entire picture can be seen in the gallery of rugs. Sheri took her creativity a step further by adding a beaded center.

Roses

These classic flowers look wonderful cascading over and around a white fence or arbor. In a minipictorial (about 12" x 14"), the best you can do is capture the impression of a rose. Assemble pink, red, and white colors in a variety of values.

Pixelate the roses in a random fashion around and over the fence. The greens are used to connect the roses. Make sure both the green stems and the roses fall across the wooden slats, so pixelate first and then hook the fence underneath.

Pixelated roses cascading over a fence, #8-cut wool on linen. Designed and hooked by Jane Halliwell Green, Edgewater, Maryland, 2008.

Pixelated gladiolas and lupines, #8-cut wool on linen. Designed and hooked by Jane Halliwell Green, Edgewater, Maryland, 2008.

Gladiolas, lupines, and hollyhocks

Hook a stem vertically with a slight bend. Remember, nothing in nature is absolutely straight. On either side of the stem, pixelate bundles of color. The more you twist the loops, the better your blossoms will look. To twist a loop, turn your wrist as you pull up the loop. Make sure the bundles are spaced unevenly as you progress up the stem. It sounds too easy, but the flowers look great up against a wall, white fence, or house. Standing alone in a field, they really do look like gladiolas or lupines.

Dye Formulas

Monet's Garden Spot Dye

Dye this formula for 1 yard of white or natural wool.

$1/8$ tsp. #728 Leaf Green
$1/8$ tsp. #725 Forest Green
$1/8$ tsp. #199 Golden Yellow
$1/8$ tsp. American Beauty

I designed this formula as a way of producing the impression of a garden without mixing materials. The garden is complete in the piece of fabric. Do not be afraid to leave white spots when you dye. The white areas will appear to be white flowers once the hooking is complete. Hook the strips in the curved shape of your garden beds. Avoid hooking straight lines. The more you bend the line, the better the final result will be. This works well for wide or fine-cut floor rugs.

Field of Flowers

This spot dye formula is designed for 1 yard of white or natural wool.

$1/128$ tsp. #338 Magenta
$1/128$ tsp. #818 Violet
$1/128$ tsp. #490 Blue
$1/16$ tsp. Canary

Follow the same set of directions as Monet's Garden and hook in the same fashion. Leave white areas. The color is pale and light.

Wild Flowers

This spot dye formula uses Majic Carpet dyes. The color is strong and contains less green than the formulas above.

$^1/_{16}$ tsp. Yellow
$^1/_{32}$ tsp. Red-violet
$^1/_{32}$ tsp. Blue-violet
$^1/_{16}$ tsp. Blue
$^1/_{32}$ tsp. Moss Green

If you want a darker version of this material, double the Yellow, Red-violet, and Blue.

Window boxes

A window box can be a wonderful addition to your pictorial design. The flowers can be baby proddy shapes or pixelated. Try baby proddy in the window box and pixelated vines down the side. Shagging is another technique for the window area. (A description of shagging is included in chapter 10.) The cut loops cascade out of the box up against the side of the building. Vary the length of the strips. The strips can be pulled forward and pressed down so they cascade outward from the window box. I was inspired to hook *Sorrento Window* as a study piece after seeing the beautiful window boxes in Sorrento, Italy. This piece is filled with prodded shapes and the long shagged tails add additional detail.

Close-up of a window box in *Sorrento Window*, 19" x 13", #3-cut wool on cotton warp cloth. Designed and hooked by Jane Halliwell Green, Edgewater, Maryland, 2008. Hooked as a study piece to illustrate techniques.

Walking the Line, # 8-cut wool on linen. Designed and hooked by Jane Halliwell Green, Edgewater, Maryland, 2008.

FLOWERING TREES

Pixelating works well for flowering trees. Dogwood trees and lilac bushes are two good choices. Select at least two values for the blossoms for variety, and when you pixelate them, scatter your pixels randomly so the tree looks realistic. Avoid blossoms that look planned; strive for a natural appearance.

VINES

"Walking the line" describes how to hook a climbing vine. Vines frequently surround window boxes and climb up walls. Hook the vine in regular loops and gently curve the line. Leave the tails hanging underneath the backing. Using the small, shaped proddy leaves, poke them underneath the hooked line, which is the vine's stem. The waist of the proddy shape is underneath the vine. Twist the leaf shapes with your fingers, and try to pull one leaf up a little lower or higher than the opposite one on the vine.

VEGETABLE GARDENS

Here are some clever ideas for your wall hangings. Be sure to think in quantity when planting your garden. Nobody eats just one ear of corn or one tomato!

Close up of cabbages in *Fisherman's Cottage*, page 47.

Fisherman's Cottage, 16" x 20", #4-cut wool on cotton warp cloth. Karlkraft design available through Harry M. Fraser Company. Hooked by Cyndra Mogayzel, Annapolis, Maryland, 2008.

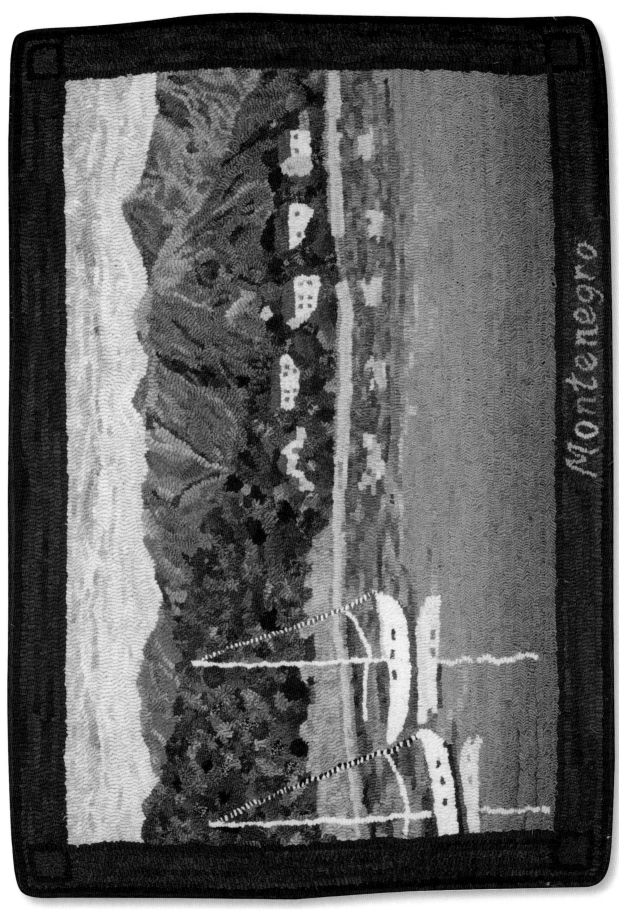

Montenegro, 30" x 22", #4-to 7- handcut wool on linen. Designed and hooked by Kathleen Bush, Silver Spring, Maryland, 2006.

Hook the dark shadows and crevices first. Then skip to the light areas, saving the medium values for last. Work from the top down and hook in the direction of the cracks. Your lines will be primarily straight. The direction should generally be vertical with some diagonal lines included. The only area where a slightly curved line should be used is at the base where the slopes are softer.

Montenegro, designed and hooked by Kathleen Bush, was based on the view from her hotel room window on the Bay of Kotor, the world's southernmost fjord, in Montenegro on the Adriatic coast. The biggest challenge was getting depth in the mountains. This task required close attention to the details. Using a variety of materials and paying special attention to the light and shadowed areas draws the viewer into the picture. The small houses nestled at the base of the mountains provide scale and a real understanding of the mountains' magnitude.

COLOR AND MATERIALS

Aerial perspective uses color to define depth and distance. With mountain groupings this is so important to keep in mind. Particles in the atmosphere make distant objects less distinct. Objects that are farther away get paler and bluer and have softer edges. The difference between the light and dark areas becomes less pronounced. The blue part of the spectrum passes through the atmosphere more easily than the red and yellow parts; therefore, we see a bluish color with distance.

In addition to aerial perspective, the season has an effect on the color of distant mountains, just as it does for trees. In winter and spring, mountains have a bluish cast; in fall, purple tones predominate. Summer hills are soft gray-greens, dulling more with distance.

Controlling values is of utmost importance and follows the same rules that apply to foreground, middle ground, and background. The hills and mountains close to the foreground are darker and warmer, getting lighter as you move backward. I would recommend, however, unless you have a very prominent mountain (which is quite uncommon in rug hooking), to always keep the values and color choices on the subdued side. If you do have a mountain in the foreground, you can use textured materials and stronger colors.

In a realistic piece, identify the direction of your light source and consider the areas that will be in shadow. One mountain can cast a shadow on another, and clouds overhead often cast shadows on mountain tops. Rarely do I use a 6- or 8-value swatch; instead, I rely on leftovers from the scrap bag and a piece of over-dyed wool.

Remember that bright materials can be over dyed with their complementary color (for example, yellow over purple, or orange over blue). Very soft light to medium blue and lavender spot dyes work as long as they are not extremely bold. At the base of the front hill or mountain, browns and greens in darker values should be added. Every mountain and hill, regardless of its shape or size, should be anchored at its base with dark values. You may suggest a tree line at the base by using dark blue-greens or violets pixelated to anchor the picture.

Snow-covered peaks are not just white. Use dip dyes: lavender and white; blue and white; gray and white; and a little blue-green and white. Place the lavender, gray, and blue hues in the shadows.

Dye formulas
Grayed Lilac Spot Dye
$1/16$ tsp. Silver Gray
$1/16$ tsp. Ocean Green
$1/16$ tsp. Aqua
$1/16$ tsp. Lavender
$1/16$ tsp. Robin's Egg Blue
Dissolve each dye in 1 cup boiling water. Spot 1 yard natural or white wool. Dissolve an additional $1/32$ tsp. Silver Gray in 1 cup water with $1/3$ cup white vinegar and pour over the entire piece of fabric. Simmer 20 to 30 minutes for a lovely, soft-gray lavender.

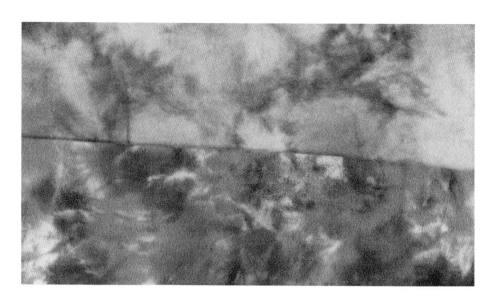

WFS #14 Granite

This bluish purple spot dye is subtle enough to use in a background mountain. It is also a wonderful addition to rocks and stone work. Dyes are dissolved in 1 cup boiling water.

Solution 1
   $^1/_{16}$ tsp. #672 Black
Solution 2
   $^1/_{64}$ tsp. #351 Red
   $^1/_{64}$ tsp. #490 Blue
   $^1/_{32}$ tsp. #119 Yellow
Solution 3
   $^1/_{32}$ tsp. #490 Blue
   $^1/_{32}$ tsp. #233 Orange

Dip Dyes

Use 4" x 6" or 4" x 8" strips for small mountains and 4" x 12" or 4" x 16" strips for large ones. Use white or natural wool, and dip the fabric in a variety of colors so you will have a selection to choose from. Each strip of wool will have one color from dark at one end to light on the other end. Aqualon blue, lavender, orchid, and myrtle green are good color choices for a mountain or hill. Start with a dye solution of $^1/_{32}$ tsp. in 1 cup boiling water. If you need to darken the strip add another $^1/_{32}$ tsp. dissolved in 1 cup water to your dye solution or directly to the dye pot. Remember that once the wool is dry, the color will be lighter.

CHAPTER 6

Roads, Streets, and Sidewalks

Long winding country roads show up frequently in our hooked designs while city streets and sidewalks are less common. Think about how to plan and hook these long, narrow, and sometimes winding shapes so you will not be traveling down the endless highway!

COUNTRY ROADS

When designing a pictorial rug, avoid wide and very long roads. Use the road to take the viewer to your focal point. When the center of interest is too small, you may find yourself looking for fillers like roads and pathways. If this seems to be the case, revisit the focal point of the picture and consider either enlarging its size or moving it so it breaks up the road. Your scene can be overpowered and the viewer's gaze taken on a joy ride simply by overdoing an element that has no real importance. Keep the rules of perspective in mind (see page 13). As the road winds from the foreground toward the horizon, it should narrow and eventually disappear. This disappearance happens at or below the horizon. If it extends above the horizon line, the road will look like a jumping ramp for water-skiers!

The color of dirt roads and the foliage along its sides change depending upon the season and the area of the country. In spring, roadsides may be covered with green grass or colorful flowers. In summer, tans and browns dominate. In fall, browns and greens are enhanced by golds and reds. In winter, soft grays, tans, and off-whites are key. If you portray a southwest landscape, the soil may need the addition of rust and reds to be realistic. Clay soils need some added tans and beiges.

As a road winds into the distance, its colors change from warm and bright in the foreground to cool and dull in the background. Brown, by the way, can be warm or cool depending upon the particular dye formula. Golden browns, for example, contain yellows and are very warm.

On the other hand, some browns have quite a bit of blue and lean toward the cooler side. In addition to controlling the intensity of colors, as you move toward the horizon, be aware that the center of the road is usually the lightest area because the sun is hitting the road here. The values become darker on the sides.

Use textured materials, spot dyes, and abrashed solids. Use a variety of materials in the foreground, limiting the number of materials in the background as you try to minimize the amount of detail. Divide the fabrics into three piles: light, medium, and dark. Take a marking pen and decide where the values will go before you start hooking. Remember, the center tends to be light and the sides much darker. Shadows will fall across the road, and these horizontal shadows add interest. The shadows also change in value as they move closer to the light. You may need to use two values for the shadow itself. If your road travels over hills, the crests are lighter than the hollows.

Finger the materials together, staggering the tails. Hook horizontally, not vertically, or your hooking will point to the sky and take the viewer right out of the picture. As you work outward from the edge of the road, maintain this horizontal direction.

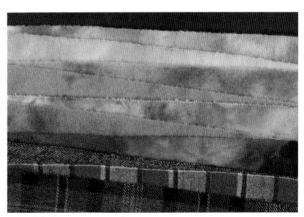

Materials for country roads.

Materials for streets and sidewalks: #1 is heather gray and is the best choice; #2 is recycled wool with some texture and is a good choice; #3 is dyed gray and is not the best choice, but it may work.

Anchor the sides of the road and break up the smooth edge with interesting grass, foliage, and branches. Use shagging and pixelating techniques if this is wall art. Always place some color along the sides of a winding road.

CITY STREETS AND SIDEWALKS

City streets need texture but not a multitude of materials. Instead, look for the lightest gray. The best material is heather gray. This is a very light gray with a textured surface. It is tough to find in local thrift shops, and rug hookers will be hoarding it if they find it. What makes it perfect is the subtle pattern on the material. Avoid medium and dark grays as they will not make a believable street. It is better to over dye some white wool with silver gray ($^1/_{32}$ tsp. over $^1/_4$ yard or an 18" x 25" piece of wool) if you need light gray, or use my basic gray formula.

Sidewalks are also created with the same light gray, but the cracks are dark and the risers are medium tones. The cracks are hooked diagonally; the risers and walks horizontally.

Sarah Province did a fabulous job in hooking this realistic pictorial, *Silver Spring Train Station, c. 1911*. She created pavement that looks like the real thing by choosing the proper materials in the correct value.

Dye Formulas (refer to the dye index for these formulas)
WFS #34 Clay Pot
Bird's Nest Spot Dye
Forest Floor
Gray

Silver Spring Train Station, c. 1911, 16" x 20", #3-cut wool on linen, designed and hooked by Sarah Province, Silver Spring, Maryland, 2006.

CHAPTER 7

Rocks

R ocks can be either the center of interest or a supporting element in a pictorial rug. Because rocks have different shapes, forms, colors, and textures, they provide a wealth of possibilities and challenges.

Rocks are infinitely variable: They can be smooth like boulders sculpted by wind and water along the shore. They can be rough with sharp edges that jut out from a bluff. They may be piled atop each other on a rock wall or scattered along a path. They are flat, angled, upright, or submerged. Decide if your rocks will be the center of interest or a minor element in the picture before you begin.

CREATING A VALUE STUDY

It helps to give yourself a road map when you are hooking rocks. Place a piece of tracing paper over your design and transfer the rock shape to the paper for a value study.

Darken the lines on your pattern so you can see them through the paper.

Rocks are divided into planes. If the values of these planes are correct, the rock will be seen as a rock; otherwise, it may resemble a blob. This is why both realistic and primitive interpretations of a scene should pay special attention to values. Outlining the exterior of the rock and filling it in will not be adequate.

Determine where the light is coming from, and with a soft pencil, shade the planes of the rock. Leave the lightest areas white. Shade the other planes either a medium or dark value. Think of a group of rocks as odd-sized boxes—they have definite tops and sides. This careful study becomes your road map for color planning and hooking. If you choose not to do the value study, use a marking pen and write notes to yourself directly on the rug backing. Hooking rocks is not difficult if you follow these guidelines.

Value study with graphite pencil. Drawing by Jane Halliwell Green, Edgewater, Maryland, 2008.

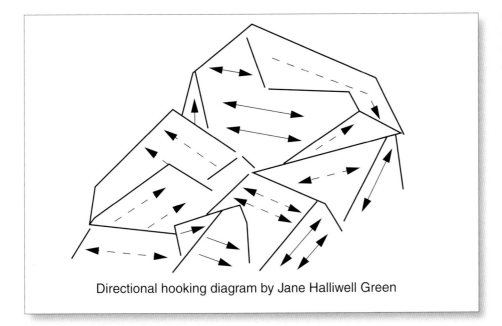

Directional hooking of rocks. Ink on paper. Drawing by Jane Halliwell Green, Edgewater, Maryland, 2008.

Directional hooking diagram by Jane Halliwell Green

COLOR AND MATERIALS

Rock colors vary greatly depending upon their geographic location, the season, and surrounding plant life. They may not be gray or brown, but instead shades of pink, blue, or purple. It helps at this stage to turn to a collection of visual aids and photographs. Take the value study a step further: use colored pencil or paint to explore how the colors really work in the rocks. The rocks in the foreground might be more intense in color, but remember that rocks are not bright, so work with a subdued palette.

Choosing the right material is the key to achieving the desired effect. Tweeds are better than plaids. A very faded plaid might work, but a wild plaid with strong multicolors will be inappropriate for a rock. My materials formula for a large prominent rock is as follows: 50 percent abrashed material, 25 percent spot dye, and 25 percent tweed. Divide these selections into three value families of light, medium, and dark. If you have difficulty placing the textured materials in a value group, pinch them between your fingers and squint to identify where they belong. See the illustration on page 59 for a good selection of fabrics.

In a small rock wall distant from the focal point, use tiny tweeds. Hook each tiny rock with different tweed. The variety of materials will provide the separation between them, and from a distance, you'll get the impression of rocks.

HOW TO HOOK ROCKS

Don't be overwhelmed by a large rocky area. Have your materials ready and your values separated into lights, mediums, and darks. Start with the largest and most prominent rock. Tackle each rock one at a time. Begin with the cracks and fissures making sure they do not look like outlines. They will look more natural if you do not use one line of hooking but vary the width and length of the cracks. Choose the value of your cracks with care. Medium values might work on the lightest planes while darker values seem unnatural.

Using your value study as a road map, begin with the lightest plane and hook in the direction of the rock's grain. Within each plane, be consistent with the direction of your hooking. Do not change direction until you start a new plane.

Each value area may include a variety of different materials, provided they are

Close up of the rocks in
Portland Head Lighthouse,
page 3.

all in the same value family. Don't be afraid of this mixing as it adds interest to the finished piece. If you add a material that doesn't belong, your eyes will tell you immediately. If you feel uncomfortable with the overall look of an area, wait until all the planes are hooked and then experiment with different fabrics. The problem is often corrected with a change in material.

Keep in mind that even rounded rocks have character, with broken slabs, cracks and lines. Few rocks are perfectly round, so if you do not want them to look like potatoes, sharpen some edges. In hooking angled rocks, the secret is to establish hard edges with unequal sides. Avoid perfect cone shapes, and keep one side longer than the next. Upright rocks often jut out of the ocean. They should have a slight lean to look natural. Take some artistic license with your pattern and punch them sideways a bit.

A close up of a rocky coast was hooked by Pam Brune. As Pam approached this

part of *Portland Head Lighthouse,* (page 3) she said, "I had to learn to hook rocks—lots and lots of rocks—and it took a long time but was a lot of fun. There were lichen and moss on the rocks near the water, and I had to look at a photograph to actually see what had been drawn on the pattern. Visual aids are so important when you are trying to hook a realistic scene."

Hooking a rock wall

Rock walls are favorite subjects. We see them all the time in country scenes, though they rarely qualify as a center of interest. Start at the top of the wall with the lightest textured material and gradually use darker textured materials as you proceed to the bottom. Hook each rock one at a time. Each rock should be a different material: do not outline in black and fill with textured wool. Don't worry about the direction of your hooking; stone walls are usually too small for direction to matter. Vary the materials so that two rocks side-by-side are not filled with

the same fabric. Each rock should be a bit different.

The last step places the darkest values and darkest rocks at the bottom. Anchor an individual rock or a group with dark shadows at their base. There is nothing worse than floating rocks, and they will rise up off the backing if you don't weigh them down. Grass or ground cover can serve as an anchor if it is very dark. Try shagging with dark greens and blues at the base, or pixelate for added texture.

Dye Formulas

Stonewall

Dissolve $1/4$ tsp. Taupe in 1 cup hot water. Add this formula to the simmering dye bath with 1 yard of natural wool. Add $1/3$ cup white vinegar. Simmer 15 minutes until the wool takes up all the color. Remove the wool, wring out excess water, and scrunch it up in a turkey roaster pan. Spot with $1/4$ tsp. Tan in $1/2$ cup hot water and $1/2$ tsp. Silver Gray in a $1/2$ cup hot water. Simmer for 30 minutes.

Over dye a selection of tans, grays, and tweeds with the above formula. Pour the Taupe, Tan, and Silver Gray into the pot at separate times. Pour the dye on top of the wool and then stir.

Materials for rocks.

CHAPTER 8

Skies

More than anything else, the sky sets the mood and time of day of your pictorial. Moreover, every other color in a rug is affected by the sky. Selecting the sky's hue is the first decision we make, but it is often the last part of the picture to be hooked.

If you are designing a landscape, you need to consider if the sky will dominate the picture and become the center of interest or if you will limit its area to no more than 25 percent of the picture. Note that it is more pleasing to the viewer to confine the sky to an area either 25 percent or 75 percent of the total picture. This avoids an even 50/50 division of sky and ground.

Choose a simple, quiet sky for a busy picture. A more reserved scene can benefit from an exciting and colorful sky. Be careful to avoid a huge sky with nothing in it.

COLOR AND MATERIALS

- Just as leaves do not always have to be green, the sky is not always blue.
- The sky is constantly changing, so don't limit yourself to one color or value. A clear sky is never the same color in its entirety. At midday it might display a touch of yellow at the horizon, merging into a cool blue and then a darker blue at the top. Use dip dyes for these gradual changes of color.
- Where the sky meets water, it is lighter. As it ascends, the sky gets darker and warmer. This change in color is due to the atmosphere (which has an even thickness of air) following the curvature of the earth. When you look directly overhead, you are looking into outer space through less atmosphere; therefore, the color of the sky is darker. When you look toward the horizon, you are viewing the scene through a thicker layer of atmosphere. In this case, the color of the sky is influenced more by the color of the atmosphere and therefore appears lighter and cooler.

- The sky is lighter than the foreground.
- Do not use very busy spot dyes in the sky. The formulas listed under the dye formulas later in this chapter are safe choices.
- Limit or eliminate tweeds and plaids in the sky. The exception is a primitive piece where anything is acceptable.
- Carry some of the sky color to the ground toward your center of interest to bring colors from the ground into the sky. This technique creates balance and ties the picture together.

> **Tip:** A great place to connect the sky to the ground is in windowpanes.

HOOKING TECHNIQUE

The primitive pictorial does not follow any rules, so its sky can be hooked vertically, horizontally, in swirling lines, or straight across. Impressionistic and realistic pictorials are more concerned with the way things look in nature and will interpret the sky differently. Kathy Hottenstein's rug, *Garden Gate*, is a good example of a primitive pictorial with a simple sky. She hooked it in swirls with one material, which is very effective.

Create movement in the sky. Skies are unpredictable and constantly changing. I am not fond of skies hooked straight across because no movement is implied. The exception is the use of a painted sky where the changing colors and clouds are already painted on the wool. In a painted sky, the dyes are applied to the wool with a paint brush prior to cutting the wool into strips. In order for the sky to look like the painted fabric, each section is cut and hooked into the sky one at a time. The hooked sky should look like the image on the fabric when you are finished. Do not cut a large quantity of strips at one time or you will lose your place. A detailed step-by-step

Garden Gate, 38" x 31", #8-cut wool on burlap. Designed by Patsy Becker. Hooked by Kathy Hottenstein, Purcellville, Virginia, 2002.

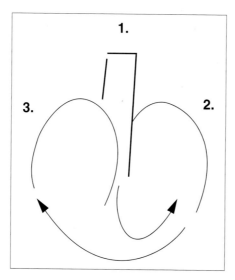

instruction for this type of sky is listed under the dye formula, Daytime Watercolor Sky, later in this chapter.

If you are not using a painted sky, starting with a straight line on either the horizon or on the top of the picture will result in straight lines throughout the entire sky. I recommend hooking in slightly curved lines. Hook the sky with a single, slightly curved line a little above the horizon—or slightly below the top of the picture. Remember, you don't want the lines to look like waves on the ocean. Continue to work either up or down from the curved line. At the top edge of the piece, some gaps will appear between the straight edge and the last curved line. Just fill in this area.

Avoid vertically hooked skies unless you are working vertically with a painted piece of fabric.

Hide the tails and create a neater edge by placing a loop, rather than a tail, on the edge of the sky area. Simply pull the tail up one space from the edge, go back to the edge and place a loop, and then work backward across the length of the sky, as illustrated above. If you dislike working backward, just hide a tail every few rows.

SKY SELECTIONS

It helps to have a visual reference when hooking a sky. Take your own photos. Collect and read painting books. Browse through local art galleries. You will see that landscape paintings are abundant. Be observant, and eventually you will be visualizing the hooked sky in your mind. The following tips and dye formulas for my favorite skies will help you on your way.

A winter daytime sky might appear ominous if snow is about to fall. This is tricky to portray because it is difficult to control the colors of snow and sky and too easy to end up with a washed-out picture. The solution is strong color. Avoid dull gray-blues. Instead, add tints of lavender and yellow near the horizon and add blue closer to the top of the picture. Choose the late afternoon when sunset colors provide strong contrasts to snow-capped houses and meadows.

Dye Formulas for Winter Skies
Cold Winter Sky
In this fabric, Silver Gray and Aqualon Blue are combined. To make the sky a bit more ominous, increase the Blue to $1/16$ tsp. This sky can make your picture appear washed out unless a strong contrast is created between it and the main design.
$1/16$ tsp. Silver Gray
$1/32$ tsp. Aqualon Blue

Dissolve the two dyes in 1 cup boiling water. Pour the solution directly on $1/2$ yard white or natural wool, using the abrash method.

Snow-Laden Sky
This dipped sky yields a winter sky with a perfect hint of color. For an interesting variation, substitute $1/32$ tsp. Lavender for the Yellow to yield a softer appearance. Use $1/2$ yard white or natural wool.
Solution 1: $1/16$ tsp. Aqualon Yellow
Solution 2: $1/16$ tsp. Robin's Egg Blue

Dissolve each dye separately in 1 cup boiling water. Prepare two simmering dye pots, each containing $1/4$ cup white vinegar. Add Blue to one pot and Yellow to the other pot. I usually add the entire cup, but you may prefer a bit less.

Dip a large section of the fabric in the Blue starting at the top where you have the selvage. Leave 2" to 3" undyed at the bottom. Lift the wool out of the pot with a wooden spoon, turn it around, and dip the white edge into the second pot. Make sure you overlap the colors. Some of the Blue section should be dipped into the yellow. If you prefer a lighter Yellow, decrease the Aqualon Yellow to $^1/_{32}$ tsp. The dark blue values will be at the top of the fabric and the yellow rests against the horizon.

> **Tip:** *When you are dyeing wool for all dipped and painted skies, it is important that the selvage of your material run the length of the wool so you will be able to cut the wool parallel to the selvage at the top. Limit the size of your fabric to $^1/_2$ yard, because anything bigger is hard to handle.*

WFS #20 Fog
This spot dye makes a good sky for a primitive piece. Dye over 1 yard white or natural wool.
Solution 1: $^1/_{128}$ *tsp. #817 Violet*
Solution 2: $^1/_{128}$ *tsp. #672 Black*
Solution 3: $^1/_{128}$ *tsp. #503 Brown*

Spring, summer, and fall skies can be brilliant blue, blue-violet, or violet—either cloudless or containing fluffy white clouds. The choice of a bright color or a subdued one depends on the contrast you wish to achieve with the objects in your picture. If the sky area is small, I tend to choose brighter colors. If my design calls for light buildings, especially white ones, then the need for medium values in the lower part of the sky is greater. The foliage may determine what looks best. Strong blues look great against the oranges, reds, and yellows of fall foliage. Using good judgment is the key to success.

Dye Formulas for Spring, Summer, and Fall Skies
Easy Daytime Sky
$^1/_8$ tsp. Robin's Egg Blue
Dissolve dye in 1 cup boiling water. Pour the solution directly onto 1 yard natural or white wool using the abrash method. This creates a light, soft sky.

Fair-Weather Daytime Sky
$^1/_4$ tsp. Sky Blue

Dissolve the dye in 1 cup boiling water. Pour the solution directly onto 1 yard natural or white wool, using the abrash method.

Dip Method: Use the same formula with $^1/_2$ yard white or natural wool. Your selvage is at the top. Prepare the simmering (never boiling) dye bath, adding about $^1/_4$ cup white vinegar to the water. Add 2 or more tablespoons of the dye solution to the dye pot (you control the color—if it looks light add another tablespoon of the solution). Wearing heavy rubber gloves and holding the wool in both hands, dip the first third of the fabric into the dye bath. Keep the wool moving up and down as you dip so you won't end up with a line between values. This edge is the dark edge, so make sure you are happy with the depth of the color. Remember that wool always dries lighter. Next dip the center of the fabric. This shade is the medium shade. By this time, only a little formula remains in the pot, so drop the rest of the wool in. The last section should be pale blue. Simmer the wool in the pot for 20 minutes to set the color.

WFS #50 Aurora Spot Dye
This spot dye is a rare one that works in a sky. Use 1 yard white or natural wool. Do not be concerned about leaving white areas because they look like clouds when hooked. Marge Barnard created the clouds in *Nubble Light* (page 64) using this fabric. Marge used only the light areas of the fabric for the clouds, which are hooked with a variety of interesting shapes.
Solution 1: $^1/_{64}$ tsp. #490 Blue + $^1/_{128}$ tsp. #672 Black dissolved in 1 cup boiling water
Solution 2: $^1/_{128}$ tsp. #413 Navy + $^1/_{128}$ tsp. #672 Black dissolved in 1 cup boiling water

New England Sky
Solution 1: $^1/_4$ tsp. Sky Blue
Solution 2: $^1/_2$ tsp. Navy Blue and $^1/_{32}$ tsp. Plum
Add the first solution to the dye pot. Add 1 yard white or natural wool. Let the

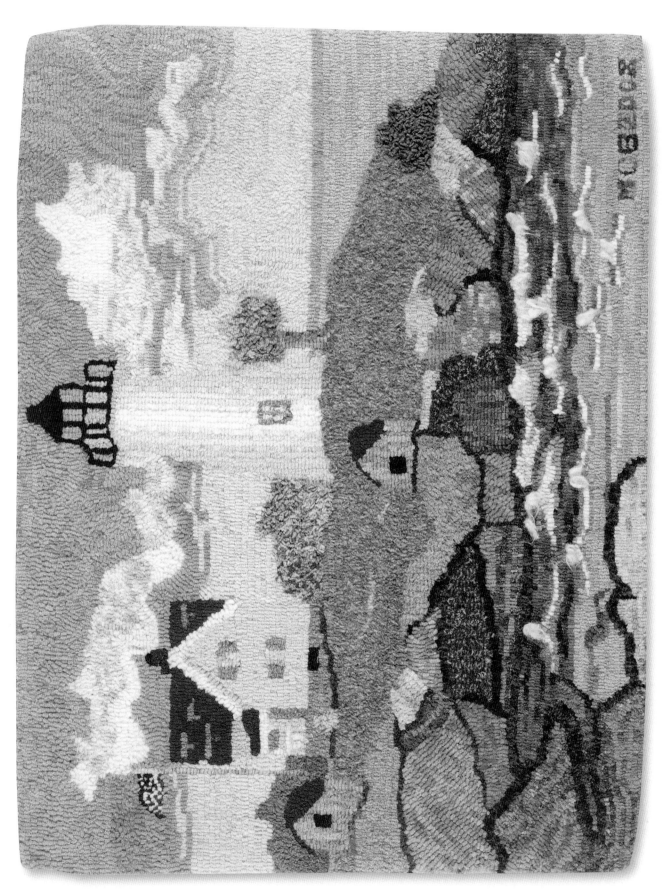

Nubble Light, 16" x 20", #3- and 4-cut wool on cotton warp cloth. Designed by Karlkraft patterns and available through Harry M. Fraser Company. Hooked by Marge Barnard, Annapolis, Maryland, 2008.

wool simmer for about 15 minutes. When most of the color has been taken up by the wool, abrash with the second solution. Use the entire cup of the second solution for a medium dark sky; use a smaller amount for a light one. By adding the second solution slowly you will control the results.

Watercolor Skies

This painted sky is hooked horizontally across the piece in gently curving lines. All the beautiful movement, shadows, and clouds are already there in the fabric. Use $1/2$ yard white wool. When you start working on this sky, make sure the selvage is at the top. Cut the wool parallel to the selvage.

Daytime Watercolor Sky

Mix each the following three solutions in 1 cup boiling water. Add $1/4$ cup white vinegar to each cup.

Solution 1: $1/32$ tsp. #490 Blue
Solution 2: $1/64$ tsp. #478 Turquoise
Solution 3: $1/16$ tsp. Lilac ($1/8$ tsp. will create a stormy look)

> **Tip:** *The secret to this sky is to use a spray bottle to control both the edges of the clouds and the value of your colors.*

1. Thoroughly soak the wool in a wetting agent and wring out the excess water.

2. Lay the wool on a 20" x 20" piece of Plexiglas (available at a local hardware store).

3. Use an inexpensive 2" or 3" flat watercolor brush and fill a spray bottle with plain water.

4. Starting at the top where you want the darkest hue, dip the brush into the #490 Blue and brush it on the fabric. You are painting the sky that will appear in your picture.

5. As you paint farther down the wool, leave white cloud shapes. As you paint, spray clean water directly on the wool around the perimeter of the clouds to soften the edges of the clouds.

Daytime Watercolor Sky.

6. Dip your brush into the blue and then in the turquoise. Clean your brush in a cup of plain water between dyes. Control the values with the spray bottle. When you spray plain water on the fabric, the dye will bleed and get lighter.

7. Put a small amount of the Lilac below the clouds as a shadow. Be careful with the Lilac or you will end up with a stormy sky.

8. Using the side of your clean brush, push some of the dye into the white cloud shapes.

9. Keep in mind: Do not use circular cloud shapes. Keep the edges irregular.

10. Use your fingers to push and pull the color. (Always wear heavy plastic gloves for this step.)

11. Pull the wool sideways until the entire piece is finished.

12. Turn the fabric over to the other side and make your best effort to repeat the colors on the back exactly where the original colors are. This step will help to saturate the wool with color and deepen the hues.

13. Fold the fabric gently and simmer with clear water and $1/4$ cup vinegar in a flat pan.

> **Tip:** *For a different look, also try ocean green, pink, and gray.*

NIGHT SKIES

When I think of night skies, Van Gogh's *Starry Night* comes to mind. Rug hookers love to hook this well-known painting in fiber. Dark blue spot dyes mixed with royal blue, violet, and navy and hooked in swirls of color like the original painting can work in a hooked night sky. The sky is the center of interest so variety is important and little attention is paid to the foreground. If you are unfamiliar with *Starry Night*, type the name of the painting into an Internet search engine and you'll see many versions appear on your computer screen.

In general, night skies must allow contrast between the objects in the picture and in the sky. The objects have to be lighter, but just slightly. Use gray materials rather than white against a nighttime sky. We often encounter the moon in these scenes, and a moon can look like a ball in the nighttime sky. Put the moon behind a cloud to avoid this circular appearance. Do not outline the moon. Clouds in a nighttime sky will be illuminated by the moon, so the closer they are to this light source, the brighter they will be.

Stormy sky, directional hooking. Ink on paper. Drawing by Jane Halliwell Green, Edgewater, Maryland, 2008.

Dye Formulas for Night Skies

Night Edge Sky

This cold sky is on the dark side. Use it for stormy weather or nighttime scenes. I call it night edge because it looks like the time of day when dark just sets in, but there is still a hint of the daylight.

Solution 1: $1/8$ tsp. #349 Fuchsia + $1/16$ tsp. #478 Turquoise (top of the wool)

Solution 2: $1/4$ tsp. Buttercup Yellow or Gold (bottom of the wool)

Slate Blue Nighttime Sky

Dissolve all three dyes in 1 cup boiling water.

$1/4$ tsp. Dark Gray

$1/4$ tsp. Blue

$1/4$ tsp. Black

Use the abrash method to dye 1 yard blue or natural wool.

Marry a variety of wool with related colors, mixing a selection of blue plaids, solids, grays, and greens with a little detergent (Tide or Ivory Snow). Simmer the colors together for 15 to 20 minutes to bleed out some of the color. If you have deep, commercially dyed blues they may bleed more and are good for this method. Rug hookers call these fabrics "bleeders." Add $1/4$ cup white vinegar to set the color.

Over dye the same bunch of materials above with a dye solution of blue or gray—$1/4$ tsp. #490 in 1 cup boiling water or $1/4$ tsp. #672 Black in 1 cup water.

WFS #23 Lilac Spot Dye for a Primitive Night Sky

Dissolve each dye in 1 cup boiling water.

Solution 1: $1/8$ tsp. #413 Navy

Solution 2: $1/8$ tsp. #672 Black

Solution 3: $1/8$ tsp. #351 Red + $1/8$ tsp. #490 Blue

STORMY SKIES

A stormy sky is a challenge to re-create in fiber. The key to success is in your choice of materials and the direction of your hooking. The materials should be on the dull side but not so flat that the sky is washed out. Three good combinations of gray, blue, and lavender are listed below.

Hook the sky in semicircles and some spirals. Draw these lines on the pattern backing or you will lose the curl. If it is raining, the direction of the rain is fan-like from the bottom of the cloud spirals.

Dye Formulas for Stormy Skies

Hook the materials randomly throughout the stormy sky. (Refer to the dye index for formula locations.)

Granite
Grayed Lilac
Abrashed Dull Blue

SUNRISE AND SUNSET

Sunrises and sunsets are my personal favorites because the color choices are enormous. Dip dyes work best here, and in the dye section, you'll see a few good selections. You are the artist in control here—if the sky is intense, as it often is at this time of day, you will pull the viewer's attention to the sky. You can end up with a softer palette by controlling the strength of the dye solutions or by choosing less intense dyes.

Sunrises are lighter and brighter and have higher clouds. They show more yellows and oranges and fewer reds and purples. If you are including the sun in a sunset, it should be lighter than any other part of your picture. Nothing can be lighter than the ultimate light source, which is the sun.

Sunrise and sunset seascapes are favorite subjects for rugs. The color of the sky must be reflected in the water, either blended into the water or hooked as a path across the water. Lynne Fowler hooked this exquisite rug, *Sunset at Racoon Point #2*. The inspiration for this piece came from the sunset seen outside Lynne's front door one evening. It is a great example of pulling the sky color effectively into the water with hooking that isn't straight; it has rhythm and movement.

Dye Formulas for Sunsets and Sunrises

Many dyes are appropriate for sunset skies. You might choose Cushing's Apricot, Crimson, Coral, Salmon, Aqualon Pink, Cardinal, Lavender, or Mulberry. I also love PRO Chemical's #233 Orange, #349 Fuchsia, and #119 Yellow. Majic Carpet dyes are intense dyes and are good choices for sunrises and sunsets.

Early Evening Sky
Solution 1: $^1/_4$ tsp. Aqualon Pink
Solution 2: $^1/_4$ tsp. Lavender
Solution 3: $^1/_4$ tsp. Aqualon Blue
Dissolve each dye separately in 1 cup boiling water and add about $^1/_4$ cup white

Sunset at Raccoon Point #2, 31$^1/_2$" x 58$^1/_2$", #9-cut wool on linen. Designed and hooked by Lynne Fowler, Oranock, Virginia, 2008.

vinegar to each cup. Use $^1/_2$ yard white or natural wool with the selvage across the top. Add the pink solution to a flat pan. Wearing heavy rubber gloves, hold the wool at one end and dip the other end into the dye bath, covering about one-third of the length with color. When the water clears, lift the wool up using a wooden spoon and pour the lavender solution into the dye pan. Holding the wool at both ends, dip the middle third of the fabric into the dye bath, overlapping the pink a bit. When the water clears add the blue solution to the pan. Grasp the pink end of the wool and dip the other end into the dye bath, overlapping the lavender a bit. After the water clears put the entire piece in the pan and simmer 20 minutes to set the color.

Lighthouse Sky
Over dye $^1/_2$ yard white or natural wool.
Solution 1: $^1/_{32}$ tsp. Canary
Solution 2: $^1/_{64}$ tsp. Cherry
Solution 3: $^1/_{32}$. tsp. Lavender
Solution 4: $^1/_{32}$ tsp. Blue
Solution 5: $^1/_{128}$ tsp. Dark Gray
Dissolve each dye in 1 cup boiling water. This process creates a sensational dipped sky. The first step is to dip the Canary. When the water clears add the Cherry to the same pan; dip, being sure to overlap the colors. In a second pan, dip the Lavender, Blue, and Gray. This can be done in one pan if you are very patient and allow each color to clear before adding another.

Mexican Sunset
Use $^1/_2$ yard of white or natural wool. Dissolve each dye in 1 cup boiling water and $^1/_4$ cup vinegar.

Solution 1: $^1/_{16}$ tsp. #119 Yellow
Solution 2: $^1/_8$ tsp. #233 Orange
Solution 3: $^1/_{16}$ tsp. #338 Magenta
Solution 4: $^1/_{32}$ tsp. Robin's Egg Blue
This is a dip dye. Start with the Yellow. Add the Orange when the Yellow is taken up by the wool, followed by the Magenta. I do the entire $^1/_2$ yard in one pan. The Robin's Egg Blue over the whole piece at the end tones it all down.

Peachy Pink Sky
Use $^1/_2$ yard white or natural wool.
Solution 1: $^1/_{32}$ tsp. Strawberry + $^1/_{32}$ tsp. #119 Yellow
Solution 2: $^1/_{16}$ tsp. #490 Blue
This very soft sky has only a touch of pink at the horizon. Use the dip dye method.

Sandy's Sky
Use $^1/_2$ yard white or natural wool.
Solution 1: $^1/_8$ tsp. #119 Yellow
Solution 2: $^1/_4$ tsp. #233 Orange
Solution 3: $^1/_8$ tsp. #338 Magenta
Solution 4: $^1/_{32}$ tsp. #490 Blue over the entire piece of wool to tone it down.
Use the dip method. This sky is extremely hot. Make enough because it is difficult to duplicate.

Diana's Watercolor Sky
Mix each dye in 1 cup boiling water with white vinegar.
Solution 1: $^1/_{16}$ tsp. #119 Yellow (start with yellow)
Solution 2: $^1/_{16}$ tsp. #233 Orange
Solution 3: $^1/_{32}$ tsp. #349 Fuchsia
Solution 4: $^1/_{32}$ tsp. #490 Blue (at the top)
Solution 5: $^1/_8$ #818 Lilac (becomes the clouds)

One word of caution about this sky: it never looks the same twice! As you paint this sky, keep the blue and orange away from each other, and the same applies to the yellow and lilac. These are complementary colors, and when two complements come together, they make gray. A little gray in your sky is okay, but if you overlap these colors many times, you will dislike the final result. Paint the blue at the top; this area is the darkest. The orange and yellow begin at the bottom of the fabric. As you work upward, add more fuchsia. The lilac makes the clouds. Lilac can be placed over the fuchsia and the blue.

CLOUDS

Although it is invisible to the naked eye, the air around us contains water vapor. When air rises, the moisture in the air cools at a high altitude and freezes into ice crystals, creating clouds. Clouds are classified by how high up in the atmosphere they occur. Slow-rising air creates sheets of clouds while fast moving air creates lumpier versions.

Clouds, like the skies they float across, also set a mood. Not only do they change colors, depending on the time of day, but they also foretell current or impending weather conditions. Although we generally focus on the common fair-weather cumulus, many other cloud types work well in pictorials. Learn their basic forms and express some of the more unusual varieties in your pictorial masterpieces.

Guidelines for hooking clouds

- If you are drawing clouds, remember to keep perspective in mind. They are larger when closer to us and smaller when far away.
- Clouds, just like foliage, have holes and caves in them where the sky peeks through.
- Clouds appear flatter when closer to the horizon.
- Hook the clouds first and the sky second.
- Hook clouds in swirling or curved lines. Do not hook clouds in straight lines.
- It is best to limit contrast between sky and clouds; a difference of one or two values is ideal. Otherwise, the clouds pop out and are too important. It is tempting when you have lots of fluffy white clouds and strong blue sky to have an imbalance here.
- Think of clouds and sky as background unless your design is mainly about the sky. These elements tie the picture together and are rarely the focal point.
- In a realistic pictorial, capture the shadows that clouds cast on the ground and on each other.
- Clouds are not 100 percent white. They reflect the color of objects above, below, and to their sides. The majority of clouds should be tinted with color, so add pink, gold, peach, and orange tints. It is the contrast of the sky color surrounding clouds that makes them appear to be white.
- Light from the sun and moon is reflected in the clouds.
- Clouds are not circles; each one has an individual shape. The edges are usually soft. Finger them into the sky.
- Dark clouds with hard edges create an angry sky.
- Clouds may be hooked diagonally rather than horizontally.
- Shadow the base of the clouds, especially cumulus clouds. This technique creates color unity. Don't overlook the shadows—they give a cloud its shape.

Cumulus clouds

Cumulus is the most common cloud formation in any artistic medium. They are pretty clouds that signal good weather. They are commonly seen in the late afternoon floating in the eastern sky opposite the setting sun. They are massive, mountainlike clouds with flat bases and rounded outlines: sometimes they appear to be sitting on an unseen shelf. Cumulus clouds are lightest near the top.

Stratus clouds

Stratus is the second most popular cloud formation. They are widely extended and look like a continuous horizontal sheet that appears to cover the sky. They lie low in the sky and forecast precipitation. These are easy clouds to hook and are a good choice for winter scenes. Be careful that you don't hook them perfectly parallel to the ground, or they will look artificial.

Cirrus clouds

Cirrus are the highest clouds, composed mostly of ice crystals and often nicknamed "mare's tails" due to their wispy, flowing contours. When rows of small cirrocumulus clouds form we see a "mackerel sky," resembling a pattern of fish scales. Use these clouds to express a windy day. They are also an excellent supporting actor in a moonlit scene. Place the moon behind them.

Nimbus clouds

Nimbus are low-hanging rain clouds. They exist in great variety and offer a multitude of dramatic and moody shapes. The bases of these clouds are not always clear, sometimes fusing with hilltops or indistinguishably merging with rain. In rug hooking they are rare because we like to depict sunny days. Occasionally our rugs show rain and the artist can hook the rain fanning out in an almost triangular shape from the bottom of this cloud. The rainy area should be slightly lighter than the background.

Dye Formulas

You need a variety of 4" x 16" dipped pieces of wool for some tinted clouds. Use either white or natural wool.

Green Tinted Clouds
$^1/_{32}$ tsp. Nile Green
Dissolve the dye in 1 cup boiling water. Follow the directions for dip dyeing on page 18–19. In all these formulas, leave one-third of the wool white.

Late Day Pink Clouds
$^1/_{32}$ tsp. Aqualon Pink

Late Day Lavender Clouds
$^1/_{32}$ tsp. Orchid

Sunny Golden Clouds
$^1/_{32}$ tsp. either Gold, Maize, or Canary (Maize will be very pale)

Lavender Gray
$^1/_{32}$ tsp. Taupe

Gray
$^1/_{32}$ tsp. #672 Black

Taupe Cloud Gradation
$^1/_4$ tsp. Taupe
Dissolve the dye in 1 cup boiling water and follow the jar dyeing method.

Gray Cloud Gradation
$^1/_4$ tsp. #672 Black
Dissolve the dye in 1 cup boiling water and follow the jar dyeing method.

FOG AND MIST

Hooking a scene in the fog is rare in fiber art but it can be done. When clouds are at ground level we call them fog or mist. To get this look in a hooked piece is a major challenge. Details of the picture will only be visible with close objects, while the background shapes will only be silhouettes without texture, strong color, or detail. The sky has to be gray or blue-gray and you must use a variety of cool and warm grays to pull it off. The only place for color is the focal point, which needs a spot of strong color. It is not uncommon to see an artist place a red boat at the focal point in a scene set in the fog.

If these sky dye formulas and the actual process of dyeing the wool itself seem to be overwhelming, I encourage you to focus on your creativity and improving your hooking skills in the beginning. Dyeing wool is an art form in itself. Refer to the resources section for sources for hand-dyed wools.

CHAPTER 9

The Supporting Cast

Y̲ou can hook almost anything into a pictorial design, which makes the supporting cast of objects for pictorial rugs endless. Certain objects are so frequently found in pictorial patterns that you will most likely include them in a rug some day.

PEOPLE

Adding figures to your pictorial design is a personal decision. When a human figure is added to the scene, it changes the entire concept of the picture. In some cases, the composition is brought to life. At other times, it can limit your viewer's imagination. A figure immediately draws the eye and can detract from your intended focal point. Here are a few suggestions.

■ Active and dramatic poses will attract more attention. Eliminating details in tiny figures is a good idea—just get the pose correct. Leave facial features to a portrait artist.

■ Keep the rules of perspective in mind. Figures are larger as they get closer. Getting the right proportions is an important part of a believable picture. A common mistake is to see the head of a figure at the roofline of a house or at the upper branches of a tree. Keep these proportions in mind: a woman is seven heads tall, a man is seven or eight heads, a child is five heads, and a toddler is three to five heads.

■ Avoid placing figures directly in the center or corners of the picture. Don't put them at the edge or looking out of the picture.

■ Overlap figures if possible.

■ Dress your figures in real clothing. Denim looks like the real thing when it is hooked. Take a close look at the real sweaters on Fran Trischmann's wall hanging, A Mother's Treasure, page 72.

■ Remember to slant the shoulders downward a bit.

■ Anchor your little standing people with a shadow, or they will float

In the rug, The Race, I agonized over hooking the horses, but I loved making the people in the stands. I call them Jane's blob people. I hooked little flesh- and light-brown-toned circles at different heights along the horizontal line in the stands (the heads). Then I added the chests to the heads. Only the upper bodies are visible and they are overlapped, which makes some individuals in the audience look like they are hugging; others appear to be looking sideways. Some of the blob people are dressed in hats, others have plaid shirts, and the ladies

Close-up of the felted sweaters in *He Who Laughs Last*, renamed *A Mother's Treasure*, page 72.

Jane's "blob people" from *The Race*, page 121.

are in pinks and purples. There are no facial features, but the viewer gets the idea. I tried to make all the clothing different without drawing attention away from the horses.

Another type of figure is a carrot person. It is the same idea as a blob person but it's used for very distant figures. Pixelate a circle and attach a carrot-shaped area, or an upside down triangle, below.

Portraits

Rug hookers often consider the human face the most difficult part to hook. That is why you see designs that depict a person whose face is covered or turned away. Sometimes in a portrait only a few facial

features are hooked into place, leaving the viewer to imagine the rest. A couple of loops for the eyes and eyebrows will be enough detail in an impressionistic portrait. A realistic portrait requires #2, #3, and #4 cuts to show all the facial features.

Fran Trischmann adapted this Beverly Conway pattern, *He Who Laughs Last*, and renamed it *A Mother's Treasure*, when she made it look like her daughters and herself. Fran tackled the facial features in this rug with confidence. We can almost describe the personalities of these fiber folks! Fran likes the look of a three-dimensional picture, and to achieve this effect, she dressed the ladies in felted sweaters that were padded and sewn on

He Who Laughs Last, renamed *A Mother's Treasure*, 24" x 36" , #4-, 6-, and 8-cut wool and felted sweaters on monk's cloth. Designed by Beverly Conway. Hooked by Fran Trischmann, Arnold, Maryland, 2007.

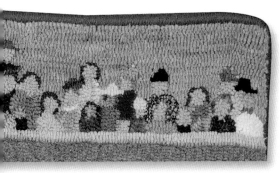

the backing. The sweaters were felted by washing them in lots of hot water and detergent. This is followed by drying them in the dryer on a high setting.

Mary Lou Bleakley designed and hooked *Wildwood Boardwalk*. It is a copy of a photograph taken on the boardwalk in Wildwood, New Jersey, of her two grandmothers, aunt, and brother Karl. Mary Lou loved seeing the people come alive in her work. The mouth on the grandmother standing to the left was a challenge. It turned down resulting in a grim expression so she changed it at the very end. Mary Lou advises that it is easier to get it right the first time.

Keep in mind the following points when tackling the challenge of hooking a realistic face:

- Hook the highlights first (on the cheeks, chin, forehead, and end of nose). Next hook the shadows in dark values. Hook medium values last.
- Be aware of the light source and place lighter shades in areas where light shines on the face.
- Add a tint to the cheeks.
- Shadows fall below the chin and hairline and beneath the upper eyelid.
- Follow the contours of the face to determine the direction of your hooking.
- Do not hook nostrils when doing a frontal view of a person; just hook the nose's highlight and the shadows on both sides.
- Keep the eyebrows light.
- Use thread or a #2 cut for upper eyelashes. Forget the lower lashes.
- Hook the eyeballs from the back of the rug to produce flat loops on the front.
- Lips can be opened or closed. The

lightest lip depends on the location of the light source. (Is it from above the face or below it?) The darkest areas around the lips are usually the corners of the mouth and the line between the upper and lower lip.

- Stay within the pattern's lines. Hook your loops low and don't pack them.
- Use multiple textured wools or yarn for the hair. Make the lines wavy or bent to create a natural look. Try the technique of shagging (page 88) the hair in a wall hanging.
- Repeat the facial colors in the person's clothing for good color balance.
- Don't panic. A large portion of the face has to be hooked before it begins to look like a real face.

Wildwood Boardwalk, 17¹/₂" x 24", #3- and 4-cut wool on linen. Designed and hooked by Mary Lou Bleakley, Arnold, Maryland, 2008.

Last Day on the Ark,
43" x 60", #3- and 4-cut wool
on cotton warp cloth.
Designed by Richard
Henderson. Hooked by
Sally Henderson, Annapolis,
Maryland, 1993.

Dye Formulas

Rug hookers are constantly in search of
the perfect formula for flesh tones. Here
are two that were shared with me years
ago and seem to do the job.

Flesh Tones #1

Dissolve all the dyes in 1 cup boiling
water. This formula calls for $1/2$ yard
white or natural wool. Divide the wool
into four pieces, each measuring about
18" x 13" and do a gradation. Start with 1
teaspoon for the first piece, 2 teaspoons
for the second piece, 4 teaspoons for the
third, and 2 or 3 tablespoons for the darkest value. You can increase or decrease
the amount of the formula to get a lighter
or darker set of flesh tones.

$3/32$ tsp. Apricot
$2/32$ tsp. Wood Rose
$1/32$ tsp. Rust
$2/32$ tsp. Salmon

Flesh Tones #2

Follow the directions under Flesh Tones
#1.

$1/16$ tsp. #338 Red
$1/32$ tsp. #119 Yellow
$1/8$ tsp. #233 Orange
$1/64$ tsp. #490 Blue
$1/64$ tsp. #672 Black

ANIMALS

Rug hookers have been including animals
in their rugs since rug hooking became
popular in the early eighteenth century.
In many cases, animals were the main
subjects on the early primitive rugs. We
love our animals, so they will always have
a prominent place in our fiber art.

Sometimes an animal is the dominant
feature of a composition, and other times
it is an accent in the landscape. Just as we
hook blob people, we can also hook blob
sheep and blob cows.

Sally Henderson's rug, *Last Day on the Ark*, was designed by her husband, Richard Henderson. Each individual animal has its own character. A sense of humor is communicated in the expressions on the faces and various poses. I like the way Sally handled the water, especially the change in color and value where the whale and shark dive underneath the surface.

Follow these tips:

- Work from a photograph. It's really difficult to get the right shape and values of color in an animal's body, especially if you are working on a large animal.
- Read the paragraphs on adding figures to your work because those principles also apply to adding animals.
- Choose the background carefully to ensure that there will be enough contrast between it and the animal. If your animal is tiny, sometimes you have to place a very distinct shadow below it to separate it from the ground cover.
- Hook in the direction you would pet the animal. Keep your lines curved.
- For a larger animal in the foreground, use textured materials. Include some dark solids to emphasize shadows around the animals' legs and underside.
- Consider using wool with a fuzzy nap. Hook the strip so that the fuzzy side is on top. I refer to it as "bunny wool," although I have also heard it referred to as "marshmallow" because it is so soft and fluffy. If nothing else, use it on bunny tails.
- Hook the animal's eyes, mouth, and nose first.
- For realistic shading use a 6- or 8-value swatch. Hook the dark and light values first, and then fill in with medium values.
- Stay in the pattern's lines. Animals can end up looking huge if you are not careful.
- Hook some of the fur from your own pet into the fur of the animal in your rug. This technique will give your rug a personal and realistic touch. If you decide to try this idea, make it your last

step and poke the fur into the rug foundation from the back side.
- A #3 cut will provide you with more room for detail, especially in the face.
- Hook whiskers with yarn. Do this step last, and put a few stitches at the end of the whiskers so they'll stand out and lay flat.
- To make a blob cow, hook a black loop, a white loop, and another black loop. Place these three loops in your background and you have a cow.
- To make a blob sheep, hook two white loops and one black loop. A #3 cut is recommended for both cows and sheep.

When dyeing wool for animal fur, work from a visual aid. Every animal is distincly colored and marked. In most cases you'll need four or five different materials.

BIRDS' NESTS

Birds' nests are a personal favorite. I like to hook the nests without the birds. The only bird I add to my pictorial designs is an impressionistic seagull, which is a curved check mark. You can see this in the sky above the wall hanging, *Sunflower Cottage*, on the back cover.

Nests come in all sizes and shapes, and so do eggs. I always start hooking the outer edge of the nest first. I complete about 1" around the top area of the nest. This area is the lightest. Then I tackle the eggs, which are sculpted. To sculpt eggs, start in the middle with the highlight and pull the loops up higher here. As you work toward the outside edge of the egg, use deeper values. Use a distinct highlight to make the eggs look round. Cut the loops and shape the egg.

After the eggs are finished, I work on hooking the nest. Materials might include eyelash yarn, tan unspun wool, regular woolen strips, string, and raffia. The front of the nest is lighter, so as I proceed to the base of the nest, I choose darker values. The area around the egg is dark, so I choose navy blue or purple to obtain depth in this area. Put the unspun wool in last and poke it in from the back. Add feathers and twigs for fun. Be careful

Funky Birds Nest, 13" x 12", #3- and 4-cut wool, feathers, yarn, and unspun wool on linen. Designed and hooked by Jane Halliwell Green, Edgewater, Maryland, 2008.

with the background—mine is a little dark. Add a bird if you are brave!

Dye Formulas

Pink Eggs Spot Dye

Use white or natural wool. This formula is good for pink eggs with burgundy spots.

Solution 1: $^1/_8$ tsp. Mulberry in 1 cup water

Solution 2: $^1/_8$ tsp. Lavender in 1 cup water

Solution 3: $^1/_4$ tsp. Rose Pink in 1 cup water

Birds Nest Spot Dye

Use white, natural, or beige wool.

Solution 1: $^1/_{16}$ tsp. Light Brown in 1 cup water

Solution 2: $^1/_{16}$ tsp. #503 Brown in 1 cup water

Cover with $^1/_{16}$ tsp. #199 Yellow in 2 cups water and simmer 20 to 30 minutes.

LETTERING

Lettering needs to be hooked clearly so it can be read easily. Letters are difficult to hook and small letters like those found on a sign post are particularly hard to do.

Before you hook, carefully write the words on your rug foundation. Leave more space between the letters than you think you need; letters seem to expand as they are hooked and will bump against each other. I always hook my initials and other sentences backward, starting with the outside edge and working toward the interior of the rug. This allows me to adjust the size of the letters as I progress.

Consider hooking letters in a finer cut of wool than you are using in the rest of your rug. For instance, use a #6 cut for the letters in a #8-cut rug. Abbreviating long words also helps with the hooking here.

VEHICLES

With vehicles, be they cars, bicycles, or trains, be sure that you have sufficient contrast between subject and the background. Hay wagons can disappear into a dirt road and boats can sink into the water if you don't plan the colors with care. Always anchor tiny objects so they don't appear to float off the surface of the scene. Plan for shadows under the tires of a car, wagon, or bicycle, and shadow the area underneath the vehicles.

BARRELS

To capture a barrel's roundness, place highlights at its top and center. As you hook toward the sides of the barrel, move from medium to dark values. Hook the barrel straps first with a dark value and then hook the areas above and below the straps with curved vertical lines. Be sure to keep your lines curved so the barrel will appear round. If necessary, establish one curved line in the middle and work backward and forward from this line. The same principles outlined for lighthouses in chapter 3 apply here.

Often barrels are stacked one on top of another and in groups of two or more stacks. To hook stacked barrels, hook the top one first with the lightest values, followed by the next one in the next darker value, and so on. The last barrels are the ones hidden in the shadows by the other barrels in the stacks. Hook these barely discernible barrels in the darkest shades.

Golden browns and weathered grays make good barrel colors; create your values by choosing textures in various shades.

BENCHES AND LAMPPOSTS

Benches and lampposts are nice accents in a park scene. Consider adding a person's silhouette on the bench for an additional point of interest. When the light within a lamppost is hooked with a soft gold, it suggests evening. Treat the lamp's globe with the same material used for creating window glass at sundown (page 38).

MORE ADDITIONS

Mailboxes, pumpkins, American flags, furniture, wallpaper, shoes, skateboards, skis, sleds, corn in the field, pigs, tractors, chickens, windmills, clotheslines, clothes, kites, baby carriages, and wagons are good additions to pictorial scenes. I'm sure you will think of a few more!

CHAPTER 10

Trees, Shrubs, and Grass

Trees reflect nature's cycle: youth, maturity, old age, and death. We identify with them. With 900 tree species in the United States, even city dwellers have their favorite trees. Rarely do we see pictorial rugs without them. The sky may be the primary mood setter in a pictorial, but trees come in second in both establishing the season and the tone of the piece. I often comment that a rug does not come to life until the trees are hooked.

DECIDUOUS TREES

Deciduous means "falling off." It is a term used to refer to trees or shrubs that lose their leaves seasonally. Most common are the deciduous trees with brightly colored fall leaves. However, many flowering spring trees are also deciduous.

Trunks

Just like people, trees have distinguishing shapes and features. Let's start with the trunk, which should be hooked first.

A telephone pole comes straight up out of the ground, but not a tree. Trunks have lots of angles to them. These angles occur naturally when branches sprout and the main trunk starts to bend in the opposite direction to balance its weight. This process continues over the years. At first glance the tree looks straight, but it really has lots of kinks in it. Trees in dense woodland tend to be more vertical, while lone trees are more angled due to the wind. The trunk narrows as it ascends, and twisting limbs are joined to it in an asymmetrical manner.

Branches must turn into twigs by the time they reach the outside edge of the tree. Limbs can be in front of the tree, and sometimes behind. This is important to recognize because the natural tendency of the untrained eye is to draw them in front. Branches also taper as they ascend. Old trees are taller and more arched than new

ones. If you are working on a primitive piece, change the pattern and give the tree a better shape.

It is important that tree trunks appear to grow into, not just rest on, the ground. This illusion can be achieved by fingering darker values into the area below the tree and carrying dark values out on either side. Shagging (see page 88) can also be effective at the base. Like every other element in a pictorial, trees will float upward if they are not grounded or shadowed at their base.

Branches

Branches are not straight, they are not the same width throughout, and they do not grow parallel to each other. Avoid putting branches opposite each other on a tree trunk; trees are not symmetrical unless they've been pruned that way. Getting this look right is a difficult task for rug hookers because we are often creating floor art that must be balanced and seen from all four sides. To create depth, make branches cross over each other. Add appropriate shadows if the branches are large enough for this amount of detail. Leave gaps for the foliage.

Color and materials for trunks and branches

Just as tree foliage is not always green, tree trunks are not always brown. Study the bark of different trees up close, not only for texture, but also for color. Look at the color of new growth and old or dead branches. Trunks may be covered with moss and fungus, so slip in some dull greens. Check your values, because a dark branch grows lighter in value as it tapers to a twig. When hooking snow scenes, wet trunks are darker than dry ones.

Because trunks are often supporting elements and should fade into the picture, reach for the medium values when color planning. Avoid both very dark and very light hues. A birch or very prominent tree in the foreground is the exception. For birch trees, choose light gray and tans with rust red and golden brown markings.

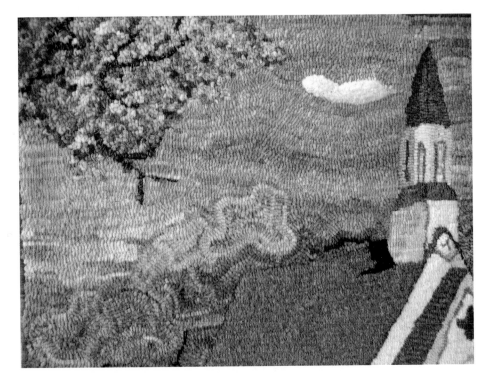

Close-up of pixelated fall tree in *New England Church*, Shown to illustrate technique.

Off-white tweed with flecks of gray may also be a good solution. Keep in mind that the lighter trunk of a birch tree necessitates a stronger color behind it, otherwise the tree will get lost. In the case of a dominant tree near or sharing the area with your focal point, bark patterns take on additional importance. Use many tweeds, over-dyed plaids, spots, and abrashed fabrics.

Tree trunks need texture. For a primitive piece, or trees in the distance, one good tweed can often suffice. Choose tweeds and plaids that are not too busy. Try combinations of brown tweeds and green plaids, or use rust brown plaids with green tweeds.

Dye Formulas

WFS #19 Stoney
$1/8$ tsp. #560 Chestnut
$1/8$ tsp. #503 Brown
Dissolve each dye in 1 cup boiling water. Squeeze 1 or 2 yards natural, beige, gray, and gold wools in a flat pan. Spot. Cover with lots of water and simmer for 20 to 30 minutes.

Stonewall
This dye makes a beautiful tree trunk as well as a rock. (See chapter 7 for this formula.)

Hooking techniques for trunks and branches

Always hook the skeleton of the tree first. The most common direction in which to hook a tree is vertically with slightly curved lines. However, when a tree trunk is wide, or in the case of a birch tree whose bark has many horizontal markings, it may be better to hook it using curved horizontal lines. This is a judgment that only you can make, and will be based on the characteristics of your particular design. Decide where the lightest area of the trunk should be. The front of the trunk is usually the lightest part, so place your light values here. Finger in your shades, remembering to stagger the tails. Then, as you work out toward the sides where the trunk curves, move from medium to dark values. Keep your light source in mind, because the sun may strike the side of the trunk and you will

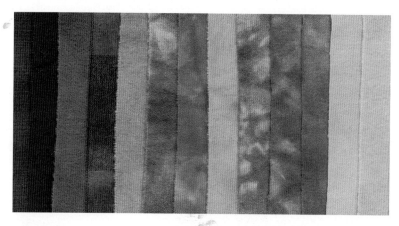

Light, medium, and dark materials to pixelate a deciduous tree.

have to adjust your values accordingly. The trunk and branches will appear cylindrical by correctly placing the light, medium, and dark values.

Leaves

Now we come to the fun stuff. Trunks are simple compared with treetops.

To begin, let's identify the overall appearance of the tree and its shape. Is the canopy shaped irregularly or like a sphere, an umbrella, a cone, or a tube? Maple trees are often oval or rounded, oaks have ragged outlines, and poplars are tall and upright. Do the branches point upward or downward? Are the leaves dense or sparse? The season also determines the tree's shape (full of leaves or bare) and also its color. Here are three wonderful ways to hook the canopy of the tree.

Note: *Three types of trees that do not lend themselves to pixelating and bundling are weeping willow, palms, and evergreens. Weeping willows are delicate trees with cascading foliage. For this kind of foliage, use a fine cut of wool (#3 and #4) and hook in slightly curved, drooping lines of one or two rows, staying inside the lines.*

Pixelating

Pixelating is a popular technique for adding texture and dimension to wall hangings. I like pixelating because it is so impressionistic. It reminds me of Seurat's paintings, where dots of color create an impression of the whole. Additional texture from a raised surface also adds to the realistic look of the foliage. At the same time, I dislike this technique because it takes a long time. When you have lots of

foliage to hook, combine techniques to add variety to your picture. Here are the steps for pixelating your tree:

1. Start by determining the light source. In most cases, such as during midday, the light source will be in the upper right of your picture. On your pattern, draw a sun with an arrow pointing toward the tree. Normally, leaves are lighter at the top of the tree and gradually get darker toward the wider and lower portion of the trunk.

2. Hook the trunk and add branches, but do not connect all of them. You want the foliage to cascade across the branches, so leave open spaces between them.

3. Choose the width of your strip. Any cut will work. On fine linen, choose a #3 or #4 cut; but if your picture is large and you are working on primitive linen, try this technique with a #8 cut. An even wider cut will yield dramatic results.

4. In this example, we will be hooking a tree in the summer. Pull a variety of greens, yellow-greens, blues, yellows, blue-greens, olive greens, and gray greens in a range of values and materials from your scrap bag. You should have plaids, tweeds, spot dyes, and solid pieces. Variety is the key. Consider adding a little yarn also.

5. Divide your materials into three piles—lights, mediums, and darks—regardless if they are solids or plaids. A word of caution: over dye any garish colors in your selections. Chartreuse can be too bright, so omit it. Emerald greens can also be toxic to your foliage unless treated in the dye pot first. Squint to see the values; a material that does not fit will stand out.

6. The pixelating stitch requires you to create twisted bundles of two or three loops and scatter them throughout the foliage. Start with the pile of light values, choose strips at random, and pixelate the light area in the tree's canopy. Some of these light fabrics will be spots; some will be solids. The colors will range from yellow-greens to blues, but they will all be light values. Pixelate some medium values in the light area for a natural look.

Light, medium, and dark values in a deciduous tree. Watercolor on paper. Painting by Jane Halliwell Green, Edgewater, Maryland, 2008.

7. As you approach the center of the tree, switch to medium values. Repeat the step above using a variety of fabrics, and add a few loops of lighter values to this area also.

8. Toward the bottom of the tree, choose mostly darks plus a few medium values. Do not put any light values at the bottom of the tree because this area is in shadow.

9. Make sure there are no dark values in the lightest areas where the sunlight hits the foliage.

10. Leave many sky holes. These are often larger near the lower part of the tree since branches near the ground are heavier and farther apart.

11. Fill the sky holes with sky color. This color should be darker, cooler, and duller than the open sky. If the sky holes are too bright, they will pop out at the viewer and look unnatural. A sky hole represents negative space and should be visually appealing. This means no circular sky holes!

12. Meander. Meandering is hooking normal loops around the pixelated bundles just to fill in spaces. When you meander, be careful to use the value compatible with the area in which you are working.

13. For the last step, flip your work over and see if you have any areas that need to be filled. The front of your work will look complete, but the back may still show large areas remaining to be hooked. If this is the case, continue to pixelate or meander.

The birds need to fly through the foliage, and pixelating makes their inclusion very easy. The advantage to the pixelating technique is the creation of more realistic exterior shapes. With small bundles of twisted loops it is easy to manipulate the irregular edges of the tree canopy.

Be sure to leave many sky holes. Rug hookers have a tendency to make the canopy of the tree too dense with leaves.

Pixelating is not just a great technique in hooking a basic tree; it allows the creation of very realistic flowering trees, such as dogwoods and crab apples. Bushes may be pixelated, and lilac bushes done this way will stand out. Flower gardens may be pixelated (refer to Chapter 4). If you need only a few loops in a strategic place, such as at the bottom of a wall or building, pixelating may be just the solution.

Pixelating Formula

- Top of the tree (in the sun): Use 75 percent light values and 25 percent medium values.
- Center of the tree (between the lights and darks): Use 60 percent medium values, 20 percent light values, and 20 percent dark values.
- Bottom of the tree (shadows): Use 75 percent dark values and 25 percent medium values.

Bundling leaves

Bundling is a better choice than pixelating if you are hooking a floor rug.

1. Start by drawing bundle shapes. These will look like jigsaw puzzle pieces with smooth edges. They don't need to be round; try scalloped shapes.

2. Start by determining the light, medium, and dark areas as done previously for pixelating.

3. Label the bundle shapes: L for light, M for medium, and D for dark.

4. Divide your materials into three values, selecting a wide variety. If you use yarn, be sure it is rug yarn.

5. Begin to fill in the light bundles. Work from the outside in and use materials at random from the light pile.

6. Fill in the dark bundles the same way. Add a little medium to the dark.

7. Fill in the medium value bundles. Add a little light and a little dark. Do not add dark material to the light bundle, and do not add light material to the dark bundle. To do so will result in those fabrics standing out too prominently.

8. Use four to five light, medium, and dark bundles in a tree's canopy, depending on its size.

9. The final result may resemble a Van Gogh landscape. Take a final glance at your work and look for any strip that may not belong.

Proddy

Refer to chapter 4 for proddy directions and templates. Trees are dramatic when the leaves are prodded. Remember this technique is suitable only for a wall hanging.

Color and materials for foliage

The seasons determine a tree's color. In spring, colors are brighter and lighter and lean toward warm tones. Blossoming trees abound, and you can pixelate or proddy these blooms. Leaves are new and small in spring, and more sky shows between them. Summer tree foliage is denser, but it still allows the sky to peek through its upper branches. Like spring, summer hues are light and warm.

In autumn a riot of color ensues. You will see trees displaying a variety of rust reds, golds, and browns. A few may turn only one color, such as red or yellow. Remember to use a little green in an autumn scene because it is unusual to see a tree, even late in the fall, totally devoid of green. Intense fall colors require some balance. Fall foliage drops off the trees, which should be indicated by showing leaves on the ground.

In winter, the focus is on the shape of the branches. A lack of color is often overcome by adding evergreen trees.

The land and trees receive differing degrees of light from the sky according to their plane. Because a tree stands more or less upright upon a more or less flat ground, it receives less light than the flat ground. Therefore, trees are almost always darker in value than the ground. In rug hooking, both the trunks and ground cover are often hooked too dark. Controlling values is important. The area immediately at the base of the tree needs to be very dark, but as you move upward, you should choose medium and light colors.

The most overused color in a pictorial rug is the color green. It is very difficult to think past this choice, particularly when you are dealing with summer and spring tree foliage. Although there are many

shades of green that add variety to your picture, ask yourself the question: what other choices do I have? Challenge yourself to include blue, yellow, rusty red, lavender, and violet. See how creative you can be, and bypass that pile of green from time to time.

The most overused material in a tree is the spot dye. Avoid hooking an entire tree in spots. Instead include a variety of solids, tweeds, and plaids. Plaids are sensational in a tree. If it is a busy plaid, over dye it before hooking.

Dye Formulas

For these dyes, squeeze a large variety of recycled wool into a flat turkey roaster. Be sure to throw in the garish emerald greens, wild yellows, green plaids and tweeds, and beige and natural wools. Choose a medium to dark green spot dye formula and spot these wools. Cover with water and $1/3$ cup white vinegar and simmer for 20 to 30 minutes. When you wash and dry the fabrics, you will have variety within an appropriate range of values.

Jane's Green

This dye is a personal favorite that I can't live without. Use 1 yard white, natural, or light green wool, and scrunch it up in a flat pan. Spot it with the following:

Solution 1: 1 tsp. #728 Green dissolved in 1 cup boiling water

Solution 2: 1 tsp. Myrtle Green dissolved in 1 cup boiling water

Solution 3: Pour $1/16$ tsp. #672 Black dissolved in 2 cups water and $1/3$ cup white vinegar over the entire pan and simmer 20 to 30 minutes on top of the stove. I use this fabric in areas needing dark values. Jane's Green also makes a gorgeous dark background without being too busy.

A great example of bundling in *Chautauqua Lake,* page 124.

WFS # 38 Fall Foliage

Solution 1: $^1/_8$ tsp. #119 Yellow + $^1/_{128}$ tsp. #351 Red

Solution 2: $^1/_8$ tsp. #119 Yellow + $^1/_{128}$ tsp. #233 Orange

Solution 3: $^1/_8$ tsp. #119 Yellow and $^1/_{128}$ tsp. #413 Navy

TOD Formulas

I like these three formulas because I can produce three totally different greens from combining the same three dyes in different quantities. All three greens blend beautifully in any rug. Dissolve the three dyes in 1 cup boiling water. Use the jar dyeing method and the value chart in chapter 1.

TOD 17
$^1/_2$ tsp. Bronze
$^1/_{16}$ tsp. Hunter Green
$^1/_{16}$ tsp. Turquoise

TOD 18
$^1/_{16}$ tsp. Bronze
$^1/_2$ tsp. Hunter Green
$^1/_{16}$ tsp. Turquoise

TOD 19
$^1/_{16}$ tsp. Bronze
$^1/_{16}$ tsp. Hunter Green
$^1/_2$ tsp. Turquoise
$^1/_{16}$ tsp. Silver Gray

EVERGREEN (CONIFEROUS) TREES

Evergreen trees abound in our pictorial designs. There are more than 100 different types of evergreens in North America, ranging from tall trees to small bushes. Evergreens are found in the coldest regions, north of 55 degrees latitude. They grow up, instead of out, and are frequently a triangular shape. They stand apart from deciduous trees because many have needles instead of leaves. All evergreens, whether they have needles or leaves, keep their foliage all year long.

The three major coniferous trees identified by their needles are fir, spruce, and pine. Firs have needles with blunt tips; spruces have four-sided needles that are sharp; and the pine is characterized by needles that grow in bunches, wrapped together at the base. Some evergreens have branches that turn upward; others downward. Some are skinny and tall; others wide and full.

Unlike their leafy cousins, they will not announce the season unless snow rests on their branches. The needles do change color with the seasons, but this change is so subtle that we don't notice it. Although evergreens are important in all pictorial scenes, they are crucial in winter ones. We rely on the strong color of their attractive needles in snow-covered landscapes. Frequently evergreens are drawn in groups of three or more trees standing together.

Hooking an Evergreen

1. Start by hooking a broken line for the trunk. This line is also a guide to the tree's slant.

2. Hook an evergreen's curved lines, following the direction of the needle growth. Start at the top and work downward toward the base. The direction of your hooking will help to identify the type of evergreen. Jack pines, for instance, have needles that sweep upward, and a weeping spruce is characterized by drooping branches.

3. Needles have a light side and a dark side, so pay attention to the light source.

4. Some pines have dense needles and very little trunk is visible; other pines have sparse needles and you will see the trunk clearly.

5. Never place the tops of a group of evergreens at the same height.

6. Never hook a group of evergreens straight up. Some trunks will lean right; others left. Think about variety. Each tree should look a little different.

7. Overlap evergreens in a group. The trees in the back are lighter.

8. In a winter scene, add bundles of snow on top of the needles after the branches are hooked.

9. If you are working with a white-tipped dip-dyed piece of wool, the branch and snow are included in the same strip.

Colors and materials for evergreens

Evergreen trees tend to be hooked with medium and dark values of the blue-green family, but rug hookers can easily expand this palette. Use cooler blue-greens to balance the deciduous trees that are often created from a warmer palette. Evergreens, however, are not always simply blue-green. We can count on a blue spruce being blue-green, but a jack pine, for example, tends to lean toward the yellow-green family. They are yellow-green, green, blue-green, brown, blue, and vio-

let. Choose your colors based on the entire picture. Don't always reach for the same hue. If you must, mix similar values of violet and blue-green. These colors are beautiful when combined.

Remember that you can combine and mix freely any two colors if they are in the same value family. Lighter values tend to be toward the top of the tree; darker ones toward the base. Place shadows under the branches using a dark value: navy blue or deep purple are good choices. Since it is rare to see an evergreen standing alone, you may have to add shadows between overlapping trees. Remember to fade out the colors as the trees become more distant. Choose dull blue-gray or medium light lavender for these receding evergreens.

Dye Formulas
Jane's Green (see page 83)

WFS #62 Blue Spruce Spot Dye
I like the touches of brown in this blue-green spot dye. This formula is dark.
Solution 1: $^1/_4$ tsp. #560 Chestnut
Solution 2: $^1/_4$ tsp. #725 Green
Solution 3: $^1/_{16}$ tsp. #478 Turquoise
Dye over natural, white, or light green or blue.

WFS #60 Pine Spot Dye
This color includes more yellow-green but leans toward the medium values.
Solution 1: $^1/_8$ tsp. #728 Green
Solution 2: $^1/_8$ tsp. #725 Green
Solution 3: $^1/_8$ tsp. #503 Brown

Dip dyes for evergreens
Measure the length of the branch and multiply it by 4. This formula will provide an estimate of the length of the wool strip at the start. Leave one end white to indicate snow at the end. If you want to warm up the snow, tint the white end with a wash of $^1/_{32}$ tsp. Maize, Aqualon Yellow, or Champagne.

To tone down blue-greens, over dye with $^1/_{32}$ tsp. Rust or Egyptian Red dissolved in 1 cup boiling water. Add the dye slowly, as you only want to dull the

Battle Creek Cypress Swamp, 18" x 24", #4-cut wool on linen. Designed and hooked by Sally D'Albora, Rockville, Maryland, 2008.

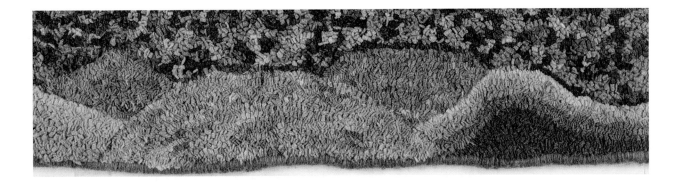

color. You may not need the entire cup. The brighter and more garish your wool, the more dye you will use to tone it down. Remember: you do not want to lose the blue-green—too much dye will change the color to mud.

FORESTS

We do see an occasional forest in the rug hooking world. The mood, colors, and values within the forest vary with the types of trees and the season. The forest has one quality that cannot be ignored: depth. Values are deeper within the trees and lighter at the edge. Don't hook every tree! Instead, show the light peeking through the trees, pay attention to the shrubs and undergrowth, control your values, and choose a variety of colors, being careful to place the strong hues in the front.

Sally D'Albora has designed this fabulous piece entitled *Battle Creek Cypress Swamp*. Sally is fascinated by trees whether bare or in full leaf. She wanted to capture this scene in wool. She used needlepoint yarn for the leaves, which allowed her to raise the loops higher and create better perspective.

Dye Formula
Forest Floor
Spot dye over white, natural, light yellow, or beige. This color makes a wonderful ground cover.
Solution 1: $^1/_2$ tsp. #199 Yellow
Solution 2: $^1/_8$ tsp. #560 Brown

SHRUBS

Bushes and shrubs are hooked in a manner similar to tree foliage. The area is smaller, but you still must pay attention to the light, medium, and dark areas and mark these on your pattern before you begin. Pixelating allows you to fit a large variety of materials into a small space and adds interest to your work. Bundling is also a good way to handle a shrub. You lose the ragged edges gained through pixelating when you choose to bundle, so use it for a bush that has been pruned.

Sculpting
Sculpting is a great way to hook shrubs, but rug hookers rarely use this technique for shrubs; it is more frequently used for flowers. The technique is suitable only for a wall hanging. Use the best materials: I prefer new wool when sculpting. To sculpt a bush:

1. Work from the inside of the bush to the outside, so you can better control the height of your loops. Hook high and pull the loops up at least 1".

2. Fill every hole, and don't forget to use a variety of materials.

3. As you get close to the edge of the shrub begin to lower your loops to $^3/_4$".

4. Pick up the scissors and cut every loop to shape the bush. You might say you are pruning the greenery! This is the fun part.

5. The sides should slope down a bit while the center of the shrub should remain higher.

Sculpting any area immediately attracts attention because it adds a three-dimensional look to your work. Because of this effect, locate sculpted areas near your rug's center of interest. Be careful not to sculpt close to the edge of your piece or you will never get the edge to lie flat.

Close-up of the sculpted edge in *New England Church*, 22" x 20", #3- and 4-cut wool on linen. Designed and hooked by Jane Halliwell Green, Edgewater, Maryland, 2002.

GRASS AND FIELDS

You might think grass would be easy to hook, but I disagree. I have tried a variety of ways to capture the look of a grassy meadow or lawn, and I am still experimenting with new ways to make this part of a pictorial piece interesting. Here is what I have learned.

If you design you own rug, limit the area covered by grass. Grass is a connecting element, along with any other ground cover, including the sky. You do not want viewers to have a first impression of an endless lawn.

Hook in slightly curved, vertical lines. This is where I want to loudly proclaim, "Do not hook grass in straight lines!" Man-made materials are straight; nature is not.

Use a limited palette of colors and limit your spot dyes. It is not uncommon to see an entire field of grass hooked using one busy spot dye. Overuse of spotted materials may result in a busy and confusing picture. Approach color by dividing the picture plane into three parts: foreground, middle ground, and background. Your colors will change as you move from front to back. If you hook the entire piece using the same material, the entire picture will be flat. Here is Jane's formula:

- Foreground: 50 percent solids with a fluctuation of values as in an abrashed piece of material, 25 percent subtle tweeds, and 25 percent spot dyes. Warmer colors like yellow, orange, and yellow-greens belong in the foreground. Over-dyed plaids can work here if they are not too busy. **Note:** *Solid does not mean flat. This is why we use the abrashed method to create our fabrics.*
- Middle ground: 75 percent abrashed solids and 25 percent tweeds. Eliminate yellows and start adding blues, blue-greens, and lavender.
- Background: 100 percent abrashed solids. Cool colors such as blue, violet, and blue-green belong in the back of your picture.
- To relieve the monotony of endless grass, reach for the complement or add flowers. See the dye formula, Monet's Garden, in chapter 4. This color mixes

beautifully with grass. Try unusual materials in a wall hanging, such as yarn, for additional texture and interest.

Shagging

Your secret weapon in the war against grass!

If you are hooking a wall hanging, this technique can add dimension to your work. Like anything else, use it in moderation. Instead of flat hooking, you will raise the loops higher and then cut them off to add vertical shapes to a flat area. This method actually yields the appearance of grass! You have two choices: raise your loops slightly ($1/4$") and cut them all off evenly, or raise the loops higher ($1/2$" to 1") and trim them unevenly. When I trim the high loops, I shape the end of the strip into a point.

You will appreciate the effect of shagging around the base of trees because it helps to ground the tree. It is natural to see weeds and grass growing around the base of a tree; our normal hooking techniques tend to be overly groomed.

Another place to use shagging is at the bottom of fence posts. Shagging adds character to a white fence when you see the vertical blades of grass, which look like the real thing, up against the rails. It also anchors the fence.

A third use for shagging is in a field where it is beneficial to break up the area visually by adding height and dimension. Do this with a subtle change in color or material. An area shagged with tiny tweeds adds interest to your picture. Notice in the wall hanging, *Maine Cottage*, that the area in the middle of the picture is raised. I have seen many individuals look at that piece and be immediately drawn to that raised area. It makes the entire picture unique and special.

Shagging can give the impression of an object in a field, particularly in a farm scene. Using the right golden brown and yellow color combinations with some added greens will yield the look of a corn field. This idea works best for a small #3- or #4-cut pictorial. You can shag with any cut from a #3 to a #8, but be aware that

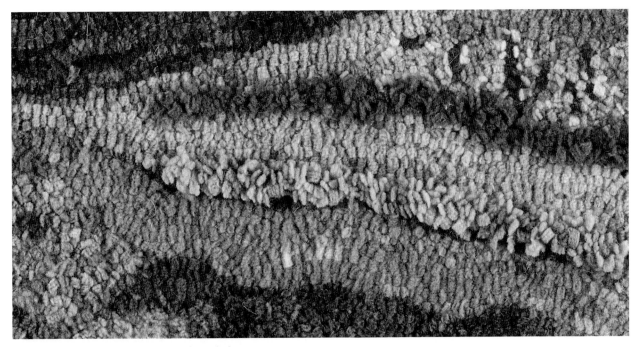

Close up of the shagging in *Maine Cottage*, below.

Maine Cottage, 12" x 14", #3-cut wool on cotton warp cloth. Designed and hooked by Jane Halliwell Green, Edgewater, Maryland.

the larger the cut, the more dramatic the results.

Dye Formulas
WFK #2 Antique Gold
Solution 1: $1/16$ tsp. #503 Brown
Solution 2: $1/16$ tsp. # 135 Yellow
Dissolve the dyes in 1 cup boiling water. Add about $1/3$ cup vinegar. Pour half the formula into the dye pot and add $1/2$ yard of white, natural, or light green wool. When the fabric begins to take up the color, pour the remaining dye solution directly on the wool to mottle it. Push the wool down into the dye bath while turning the wool and pouring. This dye technique is referred to as an abrash. It creates a beautiful green all by itself, but don't lean on this one fabric. It's a good choice for middle ground and background areas.

Placing the same formula over different base colors creates a set of different related hues that work together. This strategy is particularly helpful when color planning grass. Try $1/4$ tsp. Bronze, Olive Green, or Bronze Green dissolved in 1 cup water over base colors of beige, celery, and soft yellow.

Safari Green
Dissolve each dye in 2 cups boiling water. Spot each dye solution over 1 yard natural, white, green, beige, or yellow wool.
Solution 1: $1/4$ tsp. Bronze
Solution 2: $1/2$ tsp. Bronze Green
Solution 3: $2/32$ tsp. Bright Green
Solution 4: $1/4$ tsp. Olive Green
Solution 5: $1/4$ tsp. Ecru is poured over the entire yard. Simmer for 20 to 30 minutes and enjoy.
This is a great soft spot dye, but use it sparingly.

CHAPTER 11

Water, Water Everywhere!

ater in all its forms, from the quiet pond to raging ocean waves, has always been a huge stumbling block for artists working in any medium. Capturing motion in fiber is a rug hooker's biggest challenge. A painter can achieve motion with a brush stroke, but rug hookers have the slow and cumbersome task of employing color and directional hooking to achieve the same effect.

Consider light, shadow, depth, and texture. Refer to these general guidelines as you prepare to hook your rug:
- Water is reflective and takes on the color of its surroundings.
- Water takes planning. Write down your plan. Use a marking pen to put notes and directional arrows on your rug foundation.
- Water moves, even if no wind is blowing.
- Avoid absolutely straight lines. The exception to this would be frozen water.
- Water is transparent and reflects its surroundings.
- Water distorts shapes.
- Water is not always blue.

COLOR AND MATERIALS

If you ask the average person what color water is, he or she will invariably say blue, and this is the way most people depict it. In reality, water has little, if any color. We think of it as blue because it often reflects a blue sky. Water acts as a mirror, and everything around it is reflected on its surface. If you know what to look for and how to see it, you'll find beautiful patterns and colors in water. The weeds, algae, and other plants offer lots of opportunity for color variation. For this reason, never rely on just one piece of wool to cover any body of water.

The color of water is dependent upon geographic location. The turquoise and emerald green hues seen in the water at Cancún, Mexico, are much different from the grays and violets off the coast of Portland, Maine.

Color planning advice

Start by observing the color of the sky. The larger the body of water, the greater the area of sky reflected. Water is usually darker than the sky, so put some of your darkest sky color in your water basket.
- If the time of day is sunrise or sunset, add warm colors to the water. The setting or rising sun often creates the appearance of a path across the water with these warm hues.
- Observe the surrounding colors—including foliage, trees, and structures—and put those colors in your water basket.
- Consider the substrates—rocks, sand, and seaweed—that may lie on the bottom of this body of water. If the body of water is shallow, put their colors in your basket.
- If it's a bright day and the sun is shining directly on the water, throw some shiny stuff into your basket. Try silver, blue, lavender, green, or gold embroidery tape.

Choosing materials

Water requires variety in the choice of color and materials. Study your selections and ask yourself if you have a variety of abrashed solids, swatches, tweeds, over-dyed plaids, and spots. The right combination of these dyed materials is important. A general rule is this: Use 50 to 60 percent abrashed solids, 25 percent subdued spots and tweeds, and over-dyed plaids for the remainder. Use 5 to 10 materials in the foreground, 2 or 3 in the middle ground, and 1 or 2 in the background. Make minor changes to this formula depending on the body of water you are hooking. A pond may require a little less variety than a river.

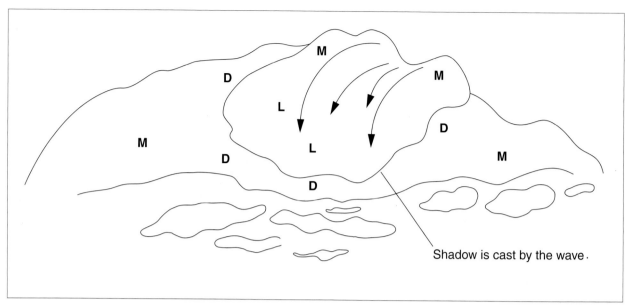

Shadow is cast by the wave.

A large wave with directional hooking and values: L = light, M = medium, and D = dark.

The biggest mistake rug artists make is to rely on only one material and one color. Variety is of utmost importance in this element, but often a large area of water will be hooked with one spot dye. Interpreting the look of water in fiber may not be perfect, but if you follow these guidelines you'll be many steps closer to a realistic interpretation.

OCEAN AND WAVES

The extreme motion of splashing, tumbling, and bouncing as ocean waves rise and fall makes ocean water particularly difficult to interpret in fiber. Hookers of primitive rugs can take artistic license with ocean waves by hooking the swells in gently rolling half-circles or circular swells. The use of spot dyes and textured materials are good choices here. A realistic interpretation of a wave, however, involves careful study and planning.

Perspective is necessary in hooking ocean water. Waves in the foreground are bold and pronounced, and their size dramatically decreases as you move toward the horizon. Waves are not all the same, so vary their height, shape, and width. Make the edges sharper near the front and round them off as you move back into the picture. Add variety in the area surrounding the waves by using a combination of different materials. Where the sky meets the water, the waves are flat.

Begin creating an ocean by marking its highlights, shadows, and medium and dark values on your rug backing. Draw a curved line on the pattern and work backward and forward from this line. You must hook the way the wave turns, starting with the whitecaps at the tip of the wave.

Think of a wave as a curving tube rolling toward you, showing its concave, usually darker, inner curve. Convex white foamy bubbles appear on the near side of the tubular curve, and the surf heads are sharp at the top edge where they turn. These white surf heads are broken and irregular. Remember that sea foam is whiter away from the shore because it isn't mixed with sand from the beach. You can use some undyed white wool here.

Complete one small area at a time, remembering to curve the lines. If you lose the curve, pull out the strip and start again. Flat lines will not show the motion that is absolutely mandatory here.

Next add the darker values at the bottom of the wave and between the swells. Medium values are hooked last and fall between the light and dark ones. You will be changing color often, as the lines of hooking tend to be short. Occasionally a jump in values will be necessary to separate one wave from another, but for the most part, avoid skipping values. Just as a dark shadow line will separate the petals

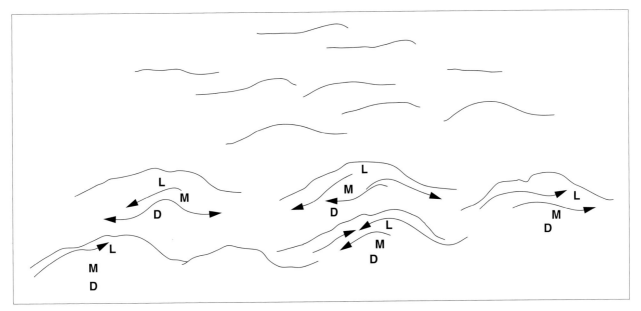

of a flower, so too will the same line break up waves.

The colors in the ocean are multiple shades of blue, green, purple, and gray. In a stormy ocean, you'll see more dull greens and blue-greens with gray whitecaps. Whatever hue is in the sky must be included in the water and is often reflected in the tips of the waves. Lastly, waves are not necessarily white, but they must appear so. Whatever you hook around the wave should provide the contrast to make it appear white.

Use all of your materials to hook ocean water. Have some dip dyes ready. The shading is built into these fabrics, but you have to control the flow of values and be committed to some cutting and piecing. Start at the tip of the wave with the light side of the dip and you will get a beautiful flow of values from light to dark. Then pick up a 6-value swatch and put some dark values at the base of the wave. After this, fill in the area with medium values.

Value changes assist in depicting movement. Combining two different swatches—for example, Value 1 from a blue-green and Value 2 from a turquoise—is called "cross-swatching." Make sure the values match, though. Sometimes Value 1 from a 6-value swatch matches Value 3 better in a second set.

Use spots and tweeds between the swells. Water flow is mainly horizontal or in the process of going that way, so you

Graphic of a swell with directional hooking. Ink on paper. Drawing by Jane Halliwell Green, Edgewater, Maryland, 2008.

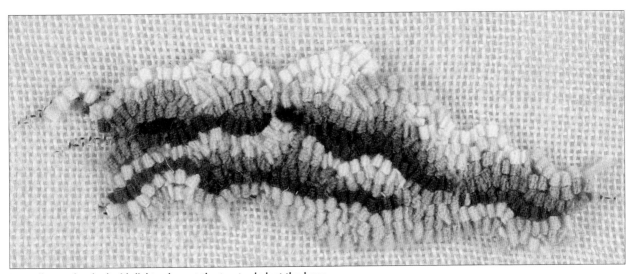

A small wave hooked with light values at the top to dark at the base.

must change the direction of your hooking to horizontal between the swells.

The same rules apply in controlling foreground, middle ground, and background with color and material choices. Play with strong bright color in the front, but include more grays as you move toward the horizon. Be sure to have enough contrast between the water and the sky at the horizon line so it is clear where one ends and the other starts.

LAKES

The moving surface of a large lake resembles the behavior of the ocean, but on a smaller scale. The waves are smaller, but the colors are similar. These smaller waves should not be hooked in one curved row. Make sure you vary the number of lines of hooking to avoid the appearance of an underline. Finger your values together. Freshwater is different from salt water, but for our purposes as fiber artists, enough similarities exist so that we can follow the same guidelines for lakes and oceans.

PONDS

Hook a pond with gently bent horizontal lines. It is imperative in any pictorial—realistic or primitive—that water be hooked with a curve to indicate motion. The still water of a pond has motion from wind blowing over its surface. You may flatten the curve as you move away from the foreground, but don't eliminate it.

Anchor the water's edge along the pond's banks with dark values. Do this with dark shadow colors in the water itself and on the banks. Work with at least one 4- or 6-value swatch, and finger the darker values from the dark edge of the pond toward the center of the body of water. Do not end the dark values abruptly. Stagger them for a natural appearance.

On the banks of the pond, add foliage, keeping the values darker along the edges. If you are creating a wall hanging try shagging and pixelating individually or in combination. Refer to chapter 10 for detailed instruction on these techniques. Your body of water will appear to float off

of your foundation if you fail to anchor the edges. Dark values add weight along the sides and hold the shape of the pond on the picture plane.

Use a variety of materials—solids, over-dyed plaids, and spots—for water. Be careful to limit those spot dyes! The color of the water should not be brighter than the sky. A pond is small and often surrounded by man-made and natural things. The colors of these objects should be added to your water—sometimes as an actual reflection and other times as only a hint of their presence. All nonfrozen water has motion, but ponds are usually more still than lakes and oceans. Because of this, the sky and cloud colors are prominently featured in ponds. Rendering the reflection of clouds in calm water is a challenge.

PUDDLES

Puddles are worth a brief mention. They are small reflective surfaces with lighter values in the center and darker values at the edges. Their surface is flat. They are not round but instead oval or irregularly shaped. The texture and values of the puddle must be in contrast to the area around it. Sometimes it is acceptable to include a little color on the surface if a nearby object provides a reflection. Think of a puddle as the pictorial's dew drop. Hook a puddle with a swatch and stay away from all other textured materials. Puddles are small, so in order to make them work, the values have to be correct.

STREAMS AND RIVERS

How we handle rivers, including the white water variety, varies depending on many factors. Some rivers are wide; others are narrow. Some run down a slope with lots of white water; others recede into the distance quietly. The shape and movement of a stream or river will affect both the color and the direction of your hooking. In fact, very different solutions are needed for each scenario. Here are general guidelines for the most common challenges:

- If you place a river or stream on your foundation, remember that its width

narrows as it retreats and its bends sharpen. This narrowing and heightened angularity results in a feeling of depth. If your pattern does not show this narrowing, redraw it.

■ Always anchor the sides of a stream or river with dark values.

■ In a quiet stream, show ripples where water and rocks meet. These ripples may form slightly irregular circular shapes. Hook the ripples in a lighter value than the water.

■ The deeper sections behave more like lakes, but in the shallow areas, you can show underwater details.

■ Colors may not be as bright, especially in streams running beneath lots of trees. The values are darker in the shadows. The opposite could be true in a quiet river running through an open marsh in the early morning. In this case, the reflection of warm, light colors in the water would be appropriate.

■ Directional hooking varies! A quiet river with little movement is hooked horizontally, even though this direction does not follow the actual flow. Hooking a slow moving body of water vertically would result in water that appears to be standing up. Moreover, vertical hooking would take the viewer right out of the picture.

■ Once again, directional hooking varies! A moving and churning white-water scene requires that you hook in the direction of the flow of the water. Hooking this type of stream can be more of a challenge than actually riding it! The lines of your hooking bend left and right and diagonally, depending on the flow. It is helpful to start in the center and work out toward the sides. Use a marking pen to draw in directional guides.

■ A final rule of thumb is necessary on directional hooking: quiet, slow-moving water can be hooked horizontally while moving, rushing water should be hooked in the direction of the water's flow.

WATERFALLS

Waterfalls range from meandering cascades tumbling down the face of a mountain to the mighty Niagara Falls. The challenge is balancing hard rock shapes in combination with falling water. To do this, the falling water has to have an interesting shape. Look for the patterns. Leonardo Da Vinci told his students to study the flow of hair in order to understand the movement of water.

■ Draw some patterns in the falls; vary the width and length.

■ Locate the area where the light hits the water. Put your highlights there, working outward from it in medium values.

■ The top of the falls is frequently brighter and lighter than the base.

■ At the base of the falls will be foam spray. Hook this with taupe, white,

Detail of *All These Things,* page 102.

ecru, and tan. White or off-white mohair yarn can be effective in small amounts to imply the spray. The area around the foam is dark and not bright, so choose blue-grays and gray in dark values.

- Anchor the sides with darker values. Take advantage of the vegetation, rocks, and trees here to frame the falls and add color and dimension to your work.
- Sometimes the falls will flow diagonally or vertically. A vertical drop is never completely straight up and down because the plummeting water is not smooth.
- Add figures to the scene to show the height of the falls and to add scale.

Dye Formulas for Water

Most of these dye formulas can be used for all types of water. Here are some general tips for dyeing wool for water:

- When using dip dyes for ocean water, measure the length of your wave and multiply by 4. This will give you a rough estimate of how long your fabric should be.
- Use a variety of dip dyes in a single scene. Make some of lighter and others darker. Wool dyed with Cushing's Copenhagen Blue and #490 PRO Chem Blue combine nicely in the same body of water. One dye is dull while the other one is bright.
- The top of the dip dye can be white-caps, but give the white area a wash in a weak solution of Taupe or Silver Gray to yield a softer color. Taupe leans toward a dull purple. If you plan to reflect a sunrise or sunset in the white-caps, try tipping the fabric with a little Coral, Salmon, Aqualon Pink, or a weak solution of Canary or #119 Yellow.
- Dip dyeing can be done over most light pastel colors.

Ocean #1
$^1/_8$ tsp. Copenhagen Blue
Dissolve in 1 cup boiling water. Dip 6"-wide pieces of wool in the formula + $^1/_4$ cup white vinegar.

Ocean #2
$^1/_8$ tsp. Sky Blue
Repeat the procedure for Ocean #1.

Ocean #3
$^1/_8$ tsp. #490 Blue
Repeat the procedure for Ocean #1.

Ocean #4
$^1/_{16}$ tsp. #478 Turquoise (very strong and bright)
Repeat the procedure for Ocean #1.

Jane's Favorite Water Formula
$^1/_2$ tsp. Aqualon Blue
$^1/_{16}$ tsp. Navy Blue
Dissolve the dyes in 1 cup boiling water. Over dye $^1/_2$-yard pieces of wool in assorted colors such as white, pink, peach, and light blue. This gives you instant variation of color in a water scene.

WFS #3 Mandarin Turquoise
This is an excellent formula for Caribbean or tropical water scenes, but use it in small amounts. Mix it with some textured material for a primitive ocean.
$^1/_2$ tsp. #490 Blue
$^1/_8$ tsp. #119 Yellow
$^1/_{32}$ tsp. #672 Black

Dissolve the dyes in 1 cup boiling water and add ¹/₂ cup white vinegar to the dye bath. Pour half the solution into the dye pot and add ¹/₂ yard white, natural, or light blue wool. Once the wool has absorbed some of the dye, gradually pour the remaining solution directly on the wool to give it a mottled look.

WFS #48 Periwinkle Spot Dye
Dissolve each dye in 1 cup water. Spot dye over 1 yard white or light blue wool. Use this dye carefully in small amounts when hooking a realistic water scene.
Solution 1: ¹/₃₂ tsp. #490 Blue
Solution 2: ¹/₃₂ tsp. #413 Navy
Solution 3: ¹/₃₂ tsp. #672 Black

WFS #53 Blue Lagoon
Dissolve each dye in 1 cup water. Spot dye over 1 yard natural or white wool. Great for tropical water.

Solution 1: ¹/₃₂ tsp. #817 Violet
Solution 2: ¹/₁₆ tsp. #478 Turquoise
Solution 3: ¹/₁₆ tsp. #425 Blue
Solution 4: ¹/₁₂₈ tsp. #233 Orange

WFS #59 Oceana
Dissolve each dye in 1 cup boiling water. Spot dye over 1 yard white or natural for tropical water.
Solution 1: ¹/₁₆ tsp. #119 Yellow and ¹/₁₂₈ tsp. #490 Blue
Solution 2: ¹/₁₆ tsp. #728 Green
Solution 3: ¹/₁₆ tsp. #725 Green

SNOW
The key to hooking snow is to remember that snow is not white: it is 75 percent color. Pure white is saved for only the brightest of highlights.

Snow reflects light the same way moving water does. If it is packed tightly in a drift, it might be almost blue. If it is fluffy

Christmas Is Coming, 16" x 20", #3- and 4-cut wool on burlap. Designed by Jane McGown Flynn. Hooked by JoAnne Bailey, North Conway, New Hampshire, 2001.

Snow Shoeing, 26" x 16", #4 to 12 hand-cut and ripped wool on linen. Designed and hooked by Susie Stephenson, Edgecomb, Maine, 2006. Photograph by Jay T. Stephenson.

and freshly fallen, it might be blue-gray or almost pink. Old snow on city streets will be gray with dirt and soot, and snowy roads are streaked with browns and grays. Gray-green and brown patches of dead grass may peek through a snowy field.

Snow has shape. On the roof it lies flat and slides toward the gutter. On fence tops and inside tree limbs, it is mounded with rounded edges. Shadows show the contours of the ground and the depth of the snow. Use a marking pen to place an X on all the areas you plan to shadow. These areas will be sharpest near the object casting the shadow, then progressively soften and dull in tone as they move farther away. Snow must be paler than the sky, and the shadows on the snow darker than the sky. Don't forget that shadows on a roof with heavy snow are just as important as those on the ground.

The sky's hues are reflected in the snow, and therefore the time of day matters when you choose your colors. It is easy to fall into the trap of always using cool colors in a snow scene. Instead, use warm yel-

lows, peaches, and pinks. The warm colors can lead the viewer's eye toward the center of interest. On a sunny day, pale yellows and oranges with blue-gray shadows are wonderful combinations.

I prefer warm skies in a cold snow scene. If you overuse the cool blues, grays, and violets, your work may end up looking dull and washed out. The warm tones add much-needed color to your picture. Take advantage of dead vegetation and evergreen trees to add color. A good trick to make snow look more brilliant is to add a spot of red. It does not have to be large, and it will grab the viewer's attention. A simple red door or American flag does the trick. JoAnne Bailey did exactly this by hooking a child wearing a red coat in the rug, *Christmas Is Coming*.

Hook most of the snow after the main element of your design is complete. Start the snow with the darkest values next to buildings, trees, and other objects. Hooking direction is determined by the wind conditions—diagonally for lots of wind and horizontally for a more peaceful effect. Like ocean water, wind can push snow around. Bend your lines to show this movement. Make sure the snow naturally mounds up against the sides of houses and trees. The whitest snow is hooked last. If you hook this pure snow first, you'll find yourself covering it up with a cloth so the lint from the other colors doesn't tint it gray.

Another way to hook snow is to sculpt it, adding dimension to your work, especially for a wall hanging. Use this technique sparingly. A little sculpting is eye-catching; too much detracts from your work.

Falling snow is simple: add it before the sky. For tiny snow flakes, pull up two tails of light gray or white and scatter them randomly throughout the sky. To draw more attention to the snow, hook a tail and one loop or pixelate the flakes.

Susie Stephenson hooked a wonderful snow scene, *Snow Shoeing* (page 90). Susie lives in Maine, and when she was a child, she snow shoed with her grandmother. She inherited snow shoes when her grandmother died and still uses them every winter. Susie says most of the snow is hooked using a pink and white blanket. She comments, "I like the way the snow is straight across the main part of the rug but following the contours to the left, and that one of the snow shoers is falling backward." Susie was successful in conveying motion, which can be difficult to achieve with a wide cut.

ICE

In contrast to fluffy bright snow, ice is dark and flat and hooked with darker values. But like snow, it reflects its surroundings, especially the sky. Ice can have a light turquoise blue, lavender, or gray cast. In the wall hanging, *Winter Wonderland* (page 100), two values of blue-gray were used for the ice. The shadow was hooked with a dark purple spot dye followed by the darker blue value. Notice that the edges of the shadow are irregular. The sky is lighter than the ice, and the horizon line is clearly evident by the shadowing at its base. The ice is hooked in absolutely straight lines, which is perfectly acceptable

Selection of materials for snow scenes. Bottom to top: plain white, Old Ivory, Aqualon Pink, Snow Spot, Pearl, and Gray.

for this nonmoving water! Notice a contrast between the sky, hooked in gently bent lines and the ice. In the front of the picture, you'll see sculpted snow banks and shagged grass. The lady has real lace sewn into her skirt, a real wool scarf, and a button placed on the back of her belt. The dog has a shagged tail made of yarn.

Dye formulas for Snow and Ice
WFS #12 Pearl
Dissolve each dye in 1 cup water. Spot dye over 1 yard white wool for great snow.
Solution 1: $1/128$ tsp. #119 Yellow
Solution 2: $1/128$ tsp. #233 Orange
Solution 3: $1/128$ tsp. #672 Black

Snow Spot #1
Use 1 yard white wool.
Solution 1: $1/64$ tsp. Aqualon Pink in 1 cup water
Solution 2: $1/64$ tsp. Orchid in 1 cup water
Solution 3: $1/128$ tsp. Aqualon Blue in 1 cup water
Solution 4: $1/64$ tsp. Aqualon Yellow in 1 cup water with $1/3$ cup white vinegar poured over all

Favorite Gray
$1/4$ tsp. #672 Black in 1 cup water
Dye values from white to dark gray using the jar or open pot method described in chapter 1.

Winter Wonderland, 18" x 16",
#3-cut, wool, yarn, and woven
fabric on cotton warp cloth.
Designed by Jane McGown
Flynn. Hooked by Jane
Halliwell Green, Edgewater,
Maryland, 2001.

Warm Snow Tones
Dye $^1/_{16}$ tsp. of any of the following Cushing dyes over $^1/_2$ yard fabric.
Silver Gray (light gray)
Old Ivory (yellow cast)
Taupe (purple cast)
Khaki (green tint)
Champagne (tan tint)

REFLECTIONS

Rug hookers often shy away from including reflections in water. Don't be intimidated; if reflections are included in your work, the scene will be more believable. Here are some basic guidelines to achieve success with this element:

Like everything else, plan the reflections and draw them on the rug foundation.

A reflection is a mirror image. In smooth water, the reflection is equal to the distance between the top and base of the object. Always measure the length of the object and make sure your reflection is of equal length.

The colors reflected should be lighter than the water and darker than the objects reflected. You can use the same material used in the real object, but over dye it for a slightly darker and less intense version than the original color. Watch the water's hue. The water is darker than the reflection!

Finger the reflection into the water so that both blend seamlessly together.

Since the reflection should be less detailed than the object it is reflecting, distort the edges of the reflection by bending the lines. The greater the movement in the water, the more distorted and wavy the lines should be. If you have an ocean with lots of movement, you should create a broken reflection. In this case, the color of the water must be inserted between the colors of the object reflected.

If the water reflects tree trunks, it also reflects the foliage.

The farther away an object is from the water, the shorter its reflection will be. As an example, a house set back from the water might only show its roof in the reflection.

Use a variety of values in the reflection.

If you are hooking a beautiful sunrise or

Fannie L. Daugherty, 32" x 36", #4-cut wool on linen. Designed and hooked by Peggy Dutton, Nanticoke, Maryland, 2007.

All These Things, 19" x 25", #3-cut wool on linen, designed and hooked by Sarah Province, Silver Spring, Maryland, 2002.

sunset, add the warm colors in the water's reflection. Hook an irregular path from the horizon toward the front of the picture. The path is wider toward the horizon. Finger these intense colors into the water.

- Lots of wind usually means no reflection. All you will see is the motion of the water.
- Still water—even dirty still water—is reflective.

BOATS

Boats are hard to draw. Use a good photo reference and practice. Do not forget that boats resting on the water will cast reflections. Boats that are moving are the exception; these boats create a wake and do not cast much of a reflection. In addition to a reflection, adding a strong shadow line visually anchors a boat. A shadow line should rest against the bottom of the boat. The shadow should not look outlined. You can avoid this unwanted effect by varying the width of the hooking.

Sailboat sails are not white. Be sure to tint them with a color. The sky is often reflected in the sails. The darker values of land and sea around your boat will make the sails appear white. Peggy Dutton did a wonderful job on her sail—even showing the patches. She hooked the skipjack, *Fannie L. Daugherty* (page 101), for her grandson, Nicholas Benton. His great-grandfather, Captain Norman Benton, oystered on Chesapeake Bay from 1969 to 1989. These boats are unique to the Chesapeake Bay, and this skipjack is one of these few remaining operating boats.

BEACHES

Many of our seascapes feature beaches in the foreground. Sometimes the beach occupies a significant amount of space; other times it is just a sliver of sand. The beach is an opportunity to add shape and color to your work. Add rocks, driftwood, grasses, seaweed, and puddles of water, sand pails, shovels, beach umbrellas, people, beach blankets, ice chests, and old row boats along the shore. Try hooking some

sea grass with raffia. In a wall hanging, use anything that provides a special effect.

Shapes come in the form of dunes and sand ripples. Hooking sand and hooking snow have many similarities. The wind pushes sand into shapes, so in order to portray the highlights and shadows accurately, use light, medium, and dark values. Wet sand can be two or three values darker than dry sand, while the insulations (ripples) may be only one value darker.

Be creative with color. Sand is unlikely to be yellow, but may be slightly gold with a gray tint. It can be a little bit pink, gray, or nearly white. Sand color is often dependent on the geography of the area. The Gulf of Mexico in Florida is known for its snow-white sand; the Atlantic beaches are gray-yellow, and the Pacific Northwest is gray. More often the colors are warm.

Be careful in choosing materials. Stay away from tweeds, and be careful in including intense spot dyes. Instead, abrashed materials work best. Sarah Province hooked *All These Things* (page 102), a wonderful beach scene of her three daughters. The title was taken from a Sunday school song: "A red and white sail boat on a blue sea / All these things you gave to me / When you made my eyes to see / Thank you God." Sarah noticed her 4-year-old daughter singing this song at the water's edge and hooked this piece as a reminder of the moment.

Dye Formulas for Sand
Dye Trick #1
Wet $1/2$-yard wool and sprinkle dry dyes on top. Simmer with $1/3$ cup vinegar. The dry dyes spread out on the wool leaving an interesting spotty effect.

Dye Trick #2
Clean your dye spoons in a jar of salt. When the salt gets very dirty, sprinkle it over $1/2$-yard white wool and simmer in the dye bath with a little white vinegar. A gray fabric with fine particulates will emerge from the dye pot and look wonderful when added to the sandy beach.

CHAPTER 12

Old Mill on the Eastern Shore

This wall hanging is an impressionistic pictorial. In July 2007 I was part of a plein air competition on the Eastern Shore of Maryland. I had three hours to find a subject and complete a painting for exhibition in the town square. I choose this old building in downtown Easton. It was a hot day, and crowds of people watched the artists work. This piece brings back these memories. The fiber version of the original painting took a few more hours to complete, but it is my favorite.

The color plan is complementary, meaning two opposite colors—blue and orange, in this case—are dominant. I choose the flag as my center of interest. The bold red and white stripes on the flag, combined with its placement left of center, should direct your eyes to its location.

The backing is regular rug linen. Most of this project was hooked with #3 and #4 cuts. If you choose, the design may be enlarged at your local copy center, placed on rug linen, and hooked with a wider strip.

TRANSFERRING THE DESIGN

I transfer my drawings to cloth using a small 12" x 19" Artograph Lightracer available through most art supply companies. See the resources section for a supplier.

Darken the lines on the pattern. They have to be bold enough to be seen through the heavy rug backing. Place the paper pattern directly on the light box. Then place the rug foundation on top of the pattern. Pin the backing to the paper if you think it might slip while you are tracing the design. Trace the design, which will be seen through the cloth. If you have trouble seeing the lines, turn off the lights in the room.

If you do not own a light box, place bridal netting, purchased at your local fabric store, over the paper pattern and trace the lines to the netting. Lay the netting on top of the rug backing. When you go over the lines with black ink, the ink will bleed through the open holes and leave enough of an impression that you can connect the lines.

Sew a zigzag stitch along the outside edge of the backing so the linen will not unravel. An alternative to stitching the edge is to place 2"-wide painter's tape on all four sides. Position the middle of the tape on the edge of the cloth and fold it forward and backward to seal the edge and reduce fraying. The tape will accomplish the same thing as a machine stitch.

Roof shadow

Hook the shadow on the right side of the roof first. It was pixelated with the darkest blues and blue-greens I could find in my scrap bag. Make sure the edges are irregular.

Roof

Start the roof by placing a few shingle shadows with a dark reddish brown spot dye. I only hooked a few. The viewer will get the idea that this is a shingle roof without excessive detail. Between the shadows, I hooked wool dyed with WFS #14 Stonewall (see chapter 3) in straight horizontal lines. The actual roof color was light gray, but I wanted some contrast against the light blue sky, so I chose a medium brown color here.

Chimney

The front side of the chimney is light and the left side dark. Hook horizontal lines in light gray for the mortar and fill in with the brick colors.

Brick house

Start the house by placing a light outline of gray around the outside of the window. Hook a few horizontal lines in medium gray to imply the presence of the mortar between the bricks. Once again, I did not hook every detail. Hook the two trellises with a medium gray. You

Old Mill on the Eastern Shore, ink on paper. Drawing by Jane Halliwell Green, Edgewater, Maryland, 2008.

want the trellis to stand out against the bricks but not look too bold. Fill in the bricks between the mortar and trellis lines using two red plaid fabrics: one dark and the other slightly lighter. Mix these two materials together at random. Refer to the section on bricks in chapter 3 for advice and dye formulas.

Flowers

Day lilies are my favorite flower. The formula that follows makes an excellent yellow orange for this summer roadside flower.

Dye Formula for Day Lilies
Red Oak PR 4A
Color 1: $1/32$ tsp. #119 Yellow dissolved in 1 cup boiling water
Color 2: $1/2$ tsp #119 Yellow + $1/4$ tsp. Fuchsia + $1/32$ tsp. #672 Black dissolved in 1 cup boiling water
Use the jar dyeing method. One tablespoon of the first color went into every jar and a regular gradation was used with the second color.

The instructions for hooking the day lilies are on the free pattern. The lightest value is #1, and #6 is the darkest. The green stamens are added before the petals. The little dots on the petals, which are a feature of this flower, are squeezed between the loops after the petals are complete.

Leaves

I hooked the leaves with pieces from my scrap bag using a variety of light blues, blue-greens, yellow-greens, and a bit of soft yellow. Keep the foliage in the foreground light because the background is dark.

Porch

A little porch is located under the flag. I used the formula WFS #34 Clay Pot (see chapter 3) to color the wool. I had to avoid the darker brick fabrics in this area in order to make the colors in the flag stand out. The area directly left of the building was hooked in a medium gray.

Old Mill on the Eastern Shore, 14" x 12", #3- to 5-cut wool on linen. Designed and hooked by Jane Halliwell Green, Edgewater, Maryland, 2008.

Tree foliage

Start pixelating the tree on the left and right sides of the building. My light values are at the top and the darker ones are up against the roofline. Be sure to leave irregular spaces for the sky color.

Background

Part of the background is the sky. This is my Daytime Watercolor Sky dye formula. Start hooking in slightly curved horizontal lines. The darkest part of your material should be at the top of the picture.

The remaining background is the negative space surrounding the lilies at the bottom of the picture. I used a dark blue abrashed fabric, Jane's Green, and a very dark blue spot dye for these areas.

Window

Hook the mullions in a medium gray and squeeze a little sky blue, green, and lily color in the window panes. The surroundings are always reflected in glass.

Flag

I usually hook my focal point first, but I saved this one until the end. The flag is a strong royal blue with a cut loop for the stars. Hook the blue first, and then squeeze in the stars. Place a white loop using a #3 cut and then cut the loop. The stars are actually the tails. Choose a bright red and an undyed white for the flag's stripes. Hook the top of the flagpole with a spot of bright gold, and finish the pole with a beige or gray.

CHAPTER 13

Finishing Thoughts

When you reach the home stretch, take a minute to evaluate your work. Listen to the comments made by fellow students. Your teacher will have valuable advice about improving parts of your picture. Don't be too hard on yourself. I always say, "There will be another day and another rug, and if I learned at least one thing from this project, it was a success." Pictorial rugs are thinking rugs and they take practice. Here are some tips on critiquing your work:

- Get off your chair and stand back from your work. Looking at those little loops only 5" from your nose won't show you how everything is working together. Put some distance between you and the rug.
- Buy a demagnifying glass at the hardware store. For a few dollars, you can purchase a peephole for a door—this is a demagnifier. Or use a pair of binoculars turned backward. A demagnifier immediately pushes you back from your work and provides a new perspective and broader view of your rug.
- Squint to eliminate detail and to see the values better.
- Turn the rug upside down. This change in perspective will distract you from the picture's story so that you can objectively evaluate balance, shapes, and color harmony.
- Stare at a point off to one side—not directly at your work—and your peripheral vision will simplify the composition.
- Look at the rug in a mirror, which reverses the shapes. Your mistakes will stand out clearly when viewed in reverse.
- Photograph your finished piece. A photograph will point to problems with values. I can always tell if my white objects are too white when I see them in a photograph.
- Color can be distracting, so change the photo to black and white on a computer. You will quickly see whether

the values in your rug are working. If they are not, the black-and-white version will look even worse than the color picture.
- Take a break and walk away from your work if you become frustrated.

HANGING A PICTORIAL RUG

If you are like me, you have struggled with hanging rugs—from wooden dowels and sewn-in sleeves to weights in the binding that hold the ends down so that the rug will hang without a curl. My friend, Irene Michaud, and her husband, came up with this method to hang and display a hooked rug. Although this works on any type of fiber art, it is particularly effective with a pictorial rug.

If you use this method, your rug will hang flat on the wall just like a painting. Moreover, if you are trying to sell your work, it is attractive to the buyer. If we, as artists, struggle with hanging rugs, you can only imagine what buyers think about this task when they purchase one of our heirlooms.

In other words, do not roll your hangings or rugs up and put them under the bed!

Irene's method for finishing and hanging hooked rugs

1. Purchase either Masonite or smooth plywood at your home improvement store. Buy 1/4" thickness for small rugs and 3/8" thickness for larger ones. The thicker the board, the heavier the weight. (I prefer the 3/8" thickness because the carpet tack strips used to mount the rug will poke through the back of a 1/4"-thick piece.)

2. Cut the Masonite or plywood exactly to the size of the rug. The store can cut it for you.

3. Purchase carpet tack strips. You will need at least two packages. The strips can be cut easily with a small coping saw.

Carpet tack strip. Photograph by Donald Green.

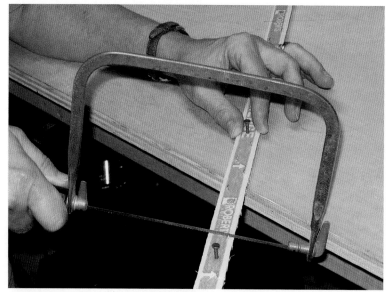

Cutting the carpet tack strip with a small band saw. Photograph by Donald Green.

4. Place the carpet tack strips $1/8$" to $1/4$" in from the edge of the wood backing all the way around. Do not skip spaces. The tacks will stick up: one side with nails and the other with tacks.

5. The arrows on the tack strips must be pointing outward. This is important because placing the nails in this direction allows them to grab your rug and keep it in its grasp when you stretch your rug over them.

6. With a hammer, tap the nails into the board.

7. If the nails come through the back of the board (this might happen with a $1/4$" board), snip them off and cover the snipped nails with heavy duct tape.

8. Attach binding tape to the edge of your last row of hooking and turn the raw edge under. You can whip the edge with yarn, but this step is unnecessary as it will not show.

9. Stretch the rug over the frame and the tacks. Start with the bottom edge, followed by the top, and then the sides. This step will not hurt or damage your rug. Do not be afraid to pull the rug tight.

10. Place a screw eye on each end of the plywood or Masonite about one-third of the way down so that it pops through to the plywood but into the area of the tack strip (the plywood is narrow and you do not want the screw eye to come out the other end). Run framing wire through the screw eyes and twist the ends securely. Use large screw eyes and heavy duty hanging wire for very large rugs (45 lb or 50 lb size).

11. It takes four mollies to hang the rug.

One note of caution about using this method. Once your larger rugs are hung this way, it is difficult to carry them with you. Smaller rugs will fit in your car, but the larger ones won't and the mounting boards are heavy. To remove and reapply the rug to the board is time-consuming, so don't mount rugs that you need to carry with you to shows or classes.

Hanging small rugs on stretcher bars

Method 1

This is another hanging system that works with small rugs under 25" all around. I use it for tiny pictorials measuring about 10" x 14".

1. Whip the edge of your work with high quality Paternayan 100 percent Persian wool yarn. In a pictorial you may have different backgrounds: sky, land, and foliage, for example. Change your yarn color as your hooked areas change. Add binding to the edge, cut off the

excess foundation, and tack the binding over the raw edge with a hem stitch.

2. Purchase stretcher bars the exact size of your finished piece. Cover the stretcher bars with wool that matches the color of your background, and staple the fabric to the bars using an industrial staple gun.

3. With thread, stitch the hooked piece to this stretched fabric.

4. On the back, add two screw eyes about one-third of the way down from the top. Run framing wire through the screw eyes, twisting the ends around tightly.

5. Hang the rug.

Method 2

Before you start hooking, sew coordinating fabric, right sides together, on the edges of your work. Hook the design. When you are finished, staple the fabric (which is really a frame for your work) to the stretcher bars prepared as in Method 1. It looks best if you can pull it tight enough to get the fabric completely around to the inside edge of the stretcher bars.

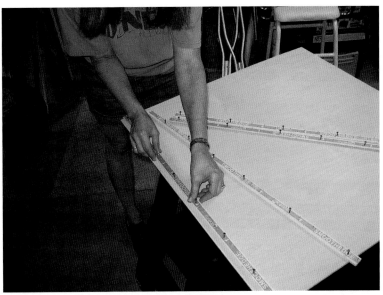

Placing the carpet tack strip ¹/₈" to ¹/₄" in from the edge of the wood backing. Photograph by Donald Green.

Cut a piece of mat board exactly the right size to fit inside the back of the stretcher bars and push it in place against the back of the hooked piece. The mat board hides the staples and is a nice finishing touch. Add screw eyes and wire to the back, and your picture is finished.

The finished wall hanging.

CHAPTER 14

A Pictorial Rug
Gallery

Sunflower, 24" x 31", # 8-cut wool on linen. Designed and hooked by Sheri DeMate, Springfield, Missouri, 2008. Photograph by Connie Costillo. Sheri's first "real" rug won Grand Champion in the state fair. The sunflower is wool appliquéd and stuffed with fiberfill. The center of the sunflower is beaded with gold and brown beads; each one is sewn on separately. A close-up of the flower can be seen in chapter 4. This is a stylistic pictorial portraying vibrant colors and great imagination.

Chesapeake Bay Marsh: New Life, 40" x 37¹/₂", #6-cut and hand-cut wool on linen. Designed and hooked by Sally D'Albora, Rockville, Maryland, 2002. This is the fourth in a series of Chesapeake Bay Designs. Sally grew up around the Chesapeake Bay. She says, "I never tire of the beautiful bay and hope to satisfy my fascination through more hooked work."

Joseph Sledding down the Hill, 32" x 23", #10 hand-cut wool on linen. Designed and hooked by Susie Stephenson, Edgecomb, Maine, 1995. Photograph by Jay T. Stephenson. In the collection of Joseph Hoyt, Edgecombe, Maine. This rug was designed from a painting the artist's son did in kindergarten. The biggest challenge was the snow: it is not completely white. It is pink, blue, and purple, depending on the light.

Cambria Gardens, 25" x 34", #3-cut wool and yarn on linen. Designed and hooked by Sarah Province, Silver Spring, Maryland, 2008. Sarah gives Roslyn Logsdon credit for helping her with this piece. The statue is hooked with light, medium, and dark values with a little extra light for highlights and some very dark for the shadows.

The Race, 31" x 31", #3-cut wool on cotton warp cloth. Designed and hooked by Jane Halliwell Green, Edgewater, Maryland, 2002. Jane used photographs and visual aids to hook the horses. A weekend workshop with Elizabeth Black got her started on the right track with the horses.

The Helicopter Rug, 23" x 24", #3- to #5-cut wool on burlap. Designed and hooked by JoAnne Bailey, North Conway, New Hampshire, 2008. JoAnne hooked this rug as a thank-you gift for the builder of her home. He took her for a helicopter ride over the state of New Hampshire. The bushes were pixelated. The interesting geometric designs in the foreground lead the viewer directly to the figure.

Main Street, 26" x 40", #3- to #6-cut wool on linen. Designed and hooked by Louise Miller, Timonium, Maryland, 2007. Main Street in Chatham, Massachusetts, on Cape Cod. Louise did a fabulous job on the bricks, which she hooked one at a time, varying the color and width of the strips to achieve depth.

Slow but Sure Wins the Race,
23" x 50", #4-cut wool on cotton
warp cloth. Designed by Richard
Henderson. Hooked by Sally
Henderson, Annapolis, Maryland,
2001. This rug is a good example of
combining a strong floral design in a
dominant border that surrounds the
picture.

Our Gang, 23³/₄" x 16¹/₂", #3-cut wool on linen. Designed by Roslyn Logsdon. Hooked by Mary Lou Bleakley, Arnold, Maryland, 2008. A family photograph of Mary Lou's three cousins and herself outside their grandmother's house in Cape May, New Jersey, became the pattern for this rug. Roslyn Logsdon was Mary Lou's teacher and simplified the hooking of the features and clothing, making the rug much easier to finish. Mary Lou feels that she captured the essence of the picture.

The Hunt, 43" x 41", #4- to 6-cut wool on monk's cloth. Designed by Emma Lou Lais. Hooked by Dorothy Sexton, Creedmoor, North Carolina, 2004. Hooking such a large background was a challenge for Dorothy. She struggled to find the right materials and not lose the details. Dorothy commented that the fox on the bottom right side kept disappearing!

The Skating Party, 36" x 20", hand-cut and ripped wool on linen. Designed and hooked by Susie Stephenson, Edgecomb, Maine, 2000. Photograph by Jay T. Stephenson. In the collection of Chuck and Becky Benton, Edgecomb, Maine. Susie's biggest challenge was to make the ice look different from the snow. To resolve this, she dyed the snow with onion skins and tea bags. She hooked the ice with an old blue and white blanket. In the end, the yellowish hues of the snow against the blue of the ice were enough contrast to separate the two elements.

Life in the Country, 36" x 24", #3-, 4-, and 6-cut wool on linen. Designed by Jeanette Fraser. Hooked by Mary Beth Hawks, Yorktown, Virginia, 2001. Photograph by Gordon Owsley. This pattern allowed Mary Beth room to personalize the design and make it her own. She did a wonderful job showing movement in the background elements of sky, hills, and grass.

You Can't Have My Wool Sweater, 22" x 36", #3- to 5-cut wool on linen. Designed by Pris Butler. Hooked by Kathy Hottenstein, Purcellville, Virginia, 2000. The sheep in this delightful wall hanging are hooked with unspun wool.

Silver Spring Train Station, c. 1911, 16" x 20", #3-cut wool on linen. Designed and hooked by Sarah Province, Silver Spring, Maryland, 2006. This pictorial is a wonderful rendition of an old train station. Light gray materials are used effectively to show the pavement outside the building.

Chautauqua Lake, 22" x 34", #5 and 6 hand-cut wool on linen. Designed and hooked by Kathleen Bush, Silver Spring, Maryland, 2006. Perspective was the biggest challenge in this piece. Kathleen says, "The lake is actually wider than it looks in the rug, but if I made the boats any smaller to indicate distance, they would have disappeared." Her favorite part is her husband's little fishing boat in the foreground.

Little Settlement, 12¹/₂" x 16", #3- and #4-cut wool, pillow top. Designed by Pearl McGown. Hooked by Pam Brune, Odenton, Maryland, 1995. Pam created this first pictorial piece with her teacher, Mary Lou Bleakley. It was her first attempt hooking textured materials; she learned that textured materials sometimes have to be cut wider to be easier to hook. She made the barn a Virginia tobacco barn.

Jack of Hearts, 36" x 24", #3- and #4-cut wool on cotton warp cloth. Designed and hooked by Jane Halliwell Green, Edgewater, Maryland, 2001. This rug was designed for the "Art of Playing Cards" exhibit, which has traveled throughout the United States the past three years. Jane's card was the jack of hearts. The entire area behind the gentleman was pixelated. This was a slow task that seemed to take forever. She had fun dressing the gentleman and placing his lady friend in the corner.

Shelter Island, 37" x 32", #3- and 4-cut wool on cotton warp cloth. Designed and hooked by Lissa Williamson, Severna Park, Maryland, 2003. The unique design features the land mass in the center surrounded by an intricate depiction of the buildings on the island.

Chesapeake Bay Marsh: Changes, 25" x 40", #6-cut and hand-cut wool on linen. Designed and hooked by Sally D'Albora, Rockville, Maryland, 2007. This detailed design is part of a series of rugs Sally is creating based upon the Chesapeake Bay area.